JEAN RHYS: A CRITICAL STUDY

JEAN RHYS

A Critical Study

Thomas F. Staley

University of Texas Press, Austin

International Standard Book Number 0-292-74014-X
Library of Congress Catalog Card Number 79-88248
Copyright © 1979 by Thomas F. Staley
All rights reserved
Printed in Great Britain

176382

To Mary McNulty Staley

Contents

Preface

The curious literary career of Jean Rhys has been touched upon frequently by the popular press and weekly reviews. The discovery and rediscovery of 'lost' writers and new-found reputations is judged newsworthy, for stories such as hers confirm the collective mythologies of the struggling figure of the writer in the modern world, and thus feature articles with full picture spreads appear in the colour supplements of the *Sunday Times* and the *Observer*. The high and low points of her bizarre life and career have been recorded and misrecorded by nearly a dozen interviewers. In England, she became for a brief time a minor cult figure, posing for fashion shots in the mass media; in America, she has been featured in 'W', the chic production of *Women's Wear Daily*, and *Ms.*[1] Lurking behind these poses of a woman in her mid-eighties commenting on clothes and her own painful hegira from the West Indies, to the provincial towns of England, half a dozen European capitals, and finally to a remote cottage in Devon, is the novelist who struggled off and on for years with her art against devastating disappointments and what seemed certain failure. These colour photographic portraits bring home to me Susan Sontag's accusation that there is something predatory in photography—the subject is somehow violated. Even with success and great age, Rhys has not escaped the image of her own fictional heroines.

Only after *Wide Sargasso Sea* was published in 1966, when she was seventy-two, and won the Smith Literary Award, did any substantial literary recognition come to her. Its success resulted in the republication of all of her novels by Andre Deutsch, and, later, the reprinting of them by Penguin, which broadened her reputation and enhanced critical acclaim to the point that A. Alvarez in the *New York Times Book Review* called her, quite simply, 'the best living English novelist'. The background of this belated attention is interesting in itself, especially in the light of the increasingly serious study of the nature of the feminine consciousness as it expresses itself in literature and of women novelists generally, but a detailed account of her life and literary reputation is not the primary task to which I have set myself.

I wrote this book with the idea that it would be the first full-length study of Jean Rhys and her work to be published. Such a prospect has obvious advantages and disadvantages. I saw it as an advantage, but I am well aware that Rhys is a writer of such enduring quality that this study is only a beginning. My aim, then, is to offer the first lines of a critical dialogue and trace with some depth her achievement. With this purpose in mind, I have not made large claims for her contribution to modern fiction, nor have I developed a thesis or confined the study to a singularity of critical or thematic approach; such undertakings as these are left to others.

As I explain in some detail later, I have attempted with mixed feelings to provide an account of the factual details of Jean Rhys's life in the first chapter, because I believe it is necessary to know something of her unusual life and especially the formative influences in order to appreciate more substantially her achievement.

I could not have put the facts of her life together even as sketchily as I have had it not been for the help of the following: John Byrne, Charles Cox, Gerry Franken, George Lawson, Anne Smyser, Oliver Stoner, and William Tilden-Smith. Above all, I am grateful to Jean Rhys herself who allowed me to ask hundreds of questions, many of which were painful for her, during two long interviews. Details of these interviews appear in an endnote to Chapter 1.

Brian Murray and R. C. Reynolds' bibliography, soon to be published in the *Bulletin of Bibliography*, was useful, and Murray's preliminary catalogue of the extensive Jean Rhys Collection at The University of Tulsa was also helpful.

My colleagues in the Graduate Faculty of Modern Letters at The University of Tulsa, Gordon Taylor and Winston Weathers, read most of the manuscript and were extremely helpful. To Darcy O'Brien and Bernard Benstock I owe special gratitude for their suggestions and insights, and to Maureen Modlish I am grateful for her intelligent help with the final draft of the manuscript. Bernice Coyle typed every word of every phase of the gestation process through to the final draft as she has done all of my work for the past nine years, and continues to raise typing to an art.

Research grants from The University of Tulsa Research Office made it possible for me to pursue work for this book in England on two different occasions. I am grateful. My students in a seminar on the 1930s posed and sometimes answered the questions that drew me to this study, and to them I will always be grateful, for I believe firmly that teaching and research enrich each other, if indeed they are not at their best one and the same.

For blunders, errors, and omissions, I am solely responsible.

August, 1978
Tulsa, Oklahoma   Thomas F. Staley

Acknowledgements

I am grateful to Andre Deutsch for permission to use copyright material from the following works of Jean Rhys:

Quartet (originally published as *Postures*)
After Leaving Mr Mackenzie
Voyage in the Dark
Good Morning, Midnight
Wide Sargasso Sea
Tigers Are Better-Looking
Sleep It Off, Lady

For permission to publish from an earlier version of Chapter 4, I am grateful to *Twentieth Century Literature* and the editor, William McBrien.

1 Art and Experience

This is a study of Jean Rhys's fiction; in this chapter, however, because of its importance, I attempt to place her life in the foreground of the entire study rather than treat it as background to her work. The extraordinary circumstances of Jean Rhys's nomadic and bohemian life are fascinating in themselves. Her origin, cultural milieu, and experiences no doubt explain many of the unique qualities of her art and must be taken into consideration in any serious treatment of her fiction. The emphasis in this chapter falls not on her later years as she has become increasingly better known, nor on her literary reputation in the fifties and sixties, which is treated in a later chapter, but upon the little known and darker time of her life prior to and during her most creative period, the twenties and thirties. Leaving aside the problematic relationship between life and art, it became clear to me from the first reading of her work that her background and culture not only set Rhys apart from her contemporary novelists, but also shaped a widely different sensibility and radical consciousness. Of vital importance to an understanding and appreciation of Rhys's contribution to the modern novel is the recognition of the striking way in which her fiction reflects a complex of values and an attitude toward life which both undercuts and opposes so many of the most cherished values, both public and private, of the bourgeois world. There is an implicit challenge in all of her work to the entire fabric of social and moral order which governs so much of society. To recognise this challenge is to begin to understand the nature of her achievement. It is necessary, then, to have some knowledge of the world she inhabited in order to more fully appreciate the world she was to create in her novels.

In her brutally honest but not infrequently humourous depiction of the isolated, abandoned, even paranoid world of her women characters who yearn vaguely for a lost beauty and passively yet doggedly attempt to survive, Rhys achieves a vital interest and importance. Her subtly rendered, complex, and revealing attitudes toward race, social classes, the bourgeois world in which her heroines

are victims, and, most important, toward women in their relationships with men and each other, come remarkably close to our
own deepest human concerns. Rhys's way of looking at the world
from the perspective of a displaced person lies at the heart of her
substantial achievement. Her imagination—at stages ironic, humourous, bitter—recreates and plays upon her experience with an
energy and daring, a pathos and wonder, that achieves substantial
meaning.

Rhys's origins bear heavily on her work. Ella Gwen Rhys
Williams was born in the West Indies on 24 August 1894, on the
island Dominica, in its capital city, Roseau. Dominica lies southern-
most of the leeward islands of the Lesser Antilles, south of
Guadeloupe and north of Martinique, just above the 15° parallel. The
first European to have set foot on the island and recorded it was
Columbus in 1493. It is an island with a tormented and bloody
history; the native Caribs fought off the European invaders for several
centuries, but once the French got a foothold they battled back and
forth with the English for over half a century, until the English finally
prevailed by 1815. During the nineteenth century Dominica passed
from a slave to a colonial society, but the dominant language of the
island remained a French patois. An island of lush vegetation and
dramatic natural beauty, it is topped by volcanic peaks between
which are carved deep gorges where rivers run through the dense
forest past coral beaches into a limpid turquoise sea. Images of this
primitive and beautiful island appear fleetingly in Rhys's novels and
finally dominate in *Wide Sargasso Sea.*

Jean Rhys was the daughter of Rhys Williams and Minna
Lockhart, the fourth of their five children. Her father was a
Welshman who had trained as a doctor at St Thomas' Hospital in
London and upon completion of his studies came to Dominica to
practice. Minna Lockhart was a third-generation Dominican Creole.
Her Creole heritage was to remain important to Jean Rhys
throughout her life and she has always felt attuned to its culture. (In
Voyage in the Dark her heroine, with the anguish of an unhappy exile,
frequently contrasts the values inherent in her native culture with the
more practical and colder, less personal, values of the English for
whom she comes to feel contempt.) As she was growing up, Jean was
not particularly close to her brothers and sisters, but white families
such as hers in the island culture lived in a confined world of narrow
dimensions crowded with family activities.[1] The family lived on the
corner of Cork and St Mary's streets in Roseau, and also maintained a

house in the mountains where Jean spent a great deal of her childhood.

While still a young girl, Jean attended a convent school staffed by Roman Catholic nuns who taught her a great deal about the Church. She was particularly fond of the Mother Superior, who had lovely black velvet eyes and whose hands were crippled with rheumatism. She told the Mother Superior that she wanted to be a nun. Her religious training at the school and her firsthand knowledge of the Negro culture through the servants became formative influences on her childhood. Some years ago in an interview she suggested how for a young girl different cultures could be joined without conflict:

> She remembers how badly she wanted to be black because 'they used to go to dances every night and they had lovely dresses, high-waisted with a belt to tuck the train through. They used to line the train with paper so it rustled, and wear gorgeous turbans. When they went to Mass we used to peer through the windows to see them.
>
> 'My father had a place in the hills called Bonavista. It was extraordinarily beautiful. I think it does something to one to be brought up in such a beautiful place, to know nothing but that. I remember things, but not when they happened. I think, was I 9 or 13? But I do remember we had this obeah woman as a cook once— obeah is the same as voodoo, but much milder. She was a rather gaudy sort of woman, very tall, and thin, and she always used to wear a red handkerchief on her wrist. She once told my fortune and a lot of it has come true.'[2]

As a young girl she was seemingly able to draw these diverse surroundings together without conflict: at fourteen she cried for the sorrows of the world and thanked Jesus for His Redemption, and she also learned to sing Negro hymns. The Dominican sunsets reminded her of Judgment Day. At the same time, the colonial mentality with its aura of superiority was very much present in her house as she grew up. Her family, for example, was not sympathetic to her interest in the Negro culture. Her mother, although she went to Church on Sunday, was also not enthusiastic about Jean's fervent devotion. Her father would give a speech that frequently began 'Buddhism is a far more beautiful religion than Christianity'. As Jean was to record much later, she had not escaped much, but she had escaped the effects of a disciplined religious upbringing, because neither of her parents was serious about formal religion. Her father's comment not only characterises his own attitude, but suggests a sense of dissatisfaction with conformity that also became part of his daughter's personality.

Even during these early years her family found her to be very private, very much to herself—her interests and curiosities a bit removed from those of the other children. In part, at least, her feelings of insecurity and passivity emerged from her adolescent fears. Her later encounters with exploitation in England and Europe, combined with the domestic and passive role expected of white women in Dominica, were sources of constant tension within her. Although she would eventually recall her years on the island with some nostalgia, she would nevertheless recognise that in both worlds masculine aggression was a common denominator, however different the form it would take. This is not to say that her anxieties were created solely by a male–female conflict, but rather that she recognised very early the conflicting and unstable role of women and how little their natures were understood by men. One day in Paris in the 1920s she went into Sylvia Beach's Shakespeare and Co. and found a book on psychoanalysis, but to her the man who wrote it was surely wrong. She hoped then that someday a man would write about women fairly—an unfulfilled hope which provided her with another impulse to write.

As she came into adolescence Jean felt unusual torment for which she could not determine the source. Out of her loneliness and isolation she began to write poetry; hers was a sensibility reflected in her favourite words 'sea', 'sleep', and 'silence'. Later in her life she would go back to this difficult period of adolescence and try to understand the source of her fears and feelings.

The passivity and turbulence, the racial mixture, the cultural contrasts between colonial and native life, all of these she absorbed with their inherent conflicts. But probably more than anything else, her early years in the West Indies formed her imagination and shaped the restlessness of her identity. Her journals which cover parts of this period record with fidelity how these experiences as a child remained a deep part of her essential being. Even amid her happy moments as a child in Dominica, she saw beneath the lazy, surface calm the continued domination of the blacks and the subordinate, reductive role that women had in this culture—the boredom and the feeling of uselessness. Boredom and domination and their effects become important themes in her fiction.

She remained in Dominica until she was sixteen; the formative years of her life were nearly complete. Her fiction was later to reveal the ambiguous feelings she carried from her childhood and adolescent years. However unresolved her feelings were when she left Dominica, they were to be sharpened by the difficulties she experienced in England. Her sense of displacement and cultural rift created a curious racial identity with blacks and an affinity for the exile. Her own attitude towards blacks as revealed in her work is complex and not easily categorised, and is further complicated by her own Creole background; but her close relationship with blacks as a child and her own experiences in what was to her the hostile world of England enabled her to understand and identify with the plight of the black immigrant who enters the alien world of white England. On a more abstract level we can see how this initial empathy created a deep sympathy for those who were outcasts, or, as Ford Madox Ford was later to put it, 'the underdog'. It was, however, the bold contrast between the West Indian culture and her life in England that gave force to her deepest feelings and thought to what would become the central themes of her fiction.

In 1910 Jean left Dominica and was not to return for twenty-five years, and then for only a short visit. She went to England and settled in Cambridge where her aunt Clarice Rhys Williams put her in the Perse School. Although the Perse School was a good one, school was not for Jean. Her interests lay elsewhere. After a term at Perse she enrolled in what is now the Royal Academy of Dramatic Art in London to study dance and acting. This period was to emerge as an important turning point in her life, and things seemed to be happening to her so quickly that she was a bit uncertain of just what to do. She was physically overwhelmed by the English climate, which nearly killed her that first winter. The drastic climatic change becomes a constant metaphor in her work to dramatise the parallel, chilling psychological effects of England. To start out on her own in England after the protected, insular life in Dominica, was a fearful experience, and one that she never quite got over.

In addition to facing the stern test of trying to find a sense of being in what had turned out to be an alien country, her sense of place was further altered by enormous changes in the life of her family in Dominica. Her father died shortly after her arrival in England, and her mother came to England in bad health. Her father had left little money, and Jean found herself suddenly completely on her own. Jean's mother was not happy that she had left school and gone to study at the RADA, but she was too ill to raise much protest, and Jean was determined to pursue a career on the stage. Given the nearly cloistered life of her childhood with its lack of any serious practical training, she felt she really had very little choice in the matter; she had to be trained to develop the natural talent she had. In short, she saw herself as she began to see so many women like her: the hapless immigrant, untrained, unsuited, and barely able to survive on one's own.

After a term at the RADA Jean signed on with a musical chorus travelling troupe. It was a number two company, which meant she performed in the smaller provincial towns in the United Kingdom. Her experiences with the troupe were similar to Anna Morgan's in *Voyage in the Dark*. She continued travelling with the troupe for two years, just prior to World War I. As an attractive young woman with beautiful green eyes, an indefinably exotic face, a delicate and well-proportioned figure, she had the appealing features for the stage. Those who knew her in the twenties and thirties have described her as striking. Had her voice been stronger and her personality more open, she might have had a successful career as an actress. After she left the troupe she took a number of theatrical jobs, playing for a time in pantomimes at the Lyceum, where she was terrified of the large rats which would suddenly appear in the cold, dank dressing rooms. As a chorus girl she played in light operas such as *Maid of the Mountains* and *Count of Luxembourg*. Although as a child she had been musical and listened to and learned the native songs that the Negroes would sing, life with a travelling chorus quickly lost its romance and must have gradually depleted her ambition.

Whatever her expectations, Jean found little glamour in this tawdry show-business world of the also-rans. Her memories are filled with the images of cheap boarding houses, mean landladies, boiled onion suppers, and bottles of gin in the dressing room—scenes she was later to recreate so well in her novels. After a year and a half of this, whatever illusions she had had disappeared. From the first, she had little confidence in her theatrical abilities; she could hide amid the chorus and dance and kick her legs, but any role which required dramatic presence was probably too much for her. Besides being young, she was shy and timid, especially before an audience.

When the company was not on tour she lived in London and found a few jobs in order to keep bread on the table. She posed as an artist's model for Adrian Allinson and also posed for advertisements; her face was once used for a Pear's Soap advertisement. Posing, modelling, dancing, moving from place to place—years later the irony of all this activity would appear; in the meantime, it was a living, and, in spite of its harsh moments, at first it had some glamour and held out a remote chance of a real career. Jean soon realised her talent in this area was limited, and her chances for any success terribly slight. As a young chorus girl she began to meet men, and what she did not learn from firsthand experience she heard from her friends in the chorus. These girls were generally attractive physically; but with little talent and almost no money, they became easy victims of male exploiters of all kinds. Naïve, with fading ambition, and almost no education, many of them became mistresses and prostitutes. Her proximity to this life is described in *Voyage in the Dark*. We can see fairly clearly one source of the bitter attitude toward men described in her novels by reflecting on these circumstances with which she was confronted so early in her life and the harsh contrast they must have presented to a young girl from such a protected environment. Her childhood images of the male figure as protector were not necessarily stable, as she records elsewhere, but however ambiguous the male figure was in her childhood, her early experience in England substantiated the malevolent qualities. These experiences also reinforced for her female dependence and male dominance as a fact of life. Male domination is intricately tied with financial dependence; hence money becomes a theme of major importance and has great psychological as well as social significance in Rhys's work. Her sense of the dependence and helplessness of the female, as we shall see in her novels, accounts in large part for the passivity of her heroines.

Life in London was transformed for Jean during the year or more that she was in love. London itself came alive, as it never had before. She felt as though something wonderful was going to happen all the time, and she lived in a state of constant excitement until the relationship turned sour and her lover broke it off. In spite of the bitter ending of this romance, she saw the man with whom she fell in love as the love of her life, not only because he was her first real love, but because she came to him with such openness and romantic readiness—at a time when, as she might have said of one of her heroines, life had not yet taken away all of her freshness. Her subsequent bitterness and disillusionment made it impossible for her ever to love with such openness and excitement again. It was in the aftermath of this loss that she began to record her experiences and feelings in a notebook. This was the first writing she had done since childhood, and as she painfully recorded her feelings, she was, unknowingly, embarking on another career which would allow her to transform the bitter experiences of her life into art. But this achievement was in the future, for these dark personal notes would lie untouched for nearly twenty years. They became the source for *Voyage in the Dark* (1934) which remains for her the favourite of her novels.

During World War I Jean continued to scratch for her existence in London. At the end of the war she met, and later married, Jean Lenglet, who was to write under the pen name Edouard de Nève. Half French and half Dutch, he had been educated by the Jesuits, but after the death of his father he ran away from home to Paris, where he took up painting and earned a meagre living as a 'chansonnier', performing in Montmartre at the *Chat Noir* and *Lapin Agile*. De Nève had a wide range of talents and an instinct for adventure. Before he met Jean he had been married and divorced, had joined the French Foreign Legion in 1914 and fought in Africa. He became a captain and was later sent to the Western Front where he was gassed. The gas damaged his lungs and its effects were to remain with him for the rest of his life. He served with the Deuxième Bureau for the French after a period of recuperation. Because of his knowledge of languages, especially German, he was sent on a number of secret missions inside Germany. His services with the Deuxième Bureau perhaps explain his presence in England on a diplomatic passport at the time Jean first met him.

After the War de Nève returned to Holland. Jean followed in 1919, and they were married there in a civil ceremony. The couple then moved to Paris, where they endured some difficult times while de Nève sought work. Because of his contacts with the Allies, de Nève eventually obtained a post with an international mission charged with the administration of post-war Vienna, working for Japanese government officials who were representatives to the mission.

The years immediately following the war were chaotic for everyone on the Continent, and for Jean they were both nerve-wracking and exciting. Amid all of the chaos and anxiety over money, she discovered she was pregnant. The pattern of the couple's life, from the day they first arrived in Paris, was one of constant movement from cheap hotel rooms and cafés, and visits to friends for a little money or at least shelter for a night or two. A child, whom they named Owen, was born in 1919, but he died three weeks after his birth. Fragments of this time in Jean's life appear throughout her work, from *The Left Bank* (1927) to *Tigers Are Better Looking* (1968).

Even when their economic situation was altered, when de Nève joined the mission, Jean suffered a great deal. She felt dislocated, fearful, and above all, isolated—feelings which were later to emerge as major themes in her novels. She sought consolation in drink—to ease the fears and uncertainties she had about other people. She was always shy and felt she did not meet people well. She felt misunderstood and many thought her aloof, but it was her shyness and caution that kept her separated from others, and she felt this loneliness deeply. The life of a vagabond was a constant strain on her nerves, too, and she developed all kinds of fears, both real and imagined. What made her nomadic life bearable was a keen sense of ironic humour which allowed her a double vision, to laugh at herself and her surroundings, while feeling, at the same time, nearly overcome with despair. This quality is reflected again in her work, and both relieves and deepens the bitter experiences of her heroines.

Vienna, Budapest, Prague, in spite of their chaotic conditions in the aftermath of the War, were exciting places where the people felt great relief to have survived—but they were also perilous places. Many people were involved in the currency exchange, which was a dangerous business, but highly profitable. To Jean this entire scene seemed mysterious, and she never really knew too much about it. In 1921 she returned for a short visit to London and discovered she was pregnant again. Her daughter, Maryvonne, was born in 1922 in Brussels, for by this time de Nève was no longer with the Allied Commission. Some of the external events of their flight from Middle-Europe are described in the short story 'Vienne'.

Jean and de Nève soon returned to Paris, moving from place to place. They gave the infant Maryvonne to the special care of a clinic in Brussels, where she remained until she was six months old. After Jean and de Nève were able to earn a bit of money—Jean worked in a dress shop and occasionally as a mannequin—their friend Germaine Richelot found a place in Paris for Maryvonne to stay until she was three.

Life in Paris during the early 1920s was no easier for Jean and de Nève than it had been when they first arrived after the War. At first de Nève tried to pursue a career in journalism, at which he had had some experience. He had connections with the Paris *Herald-Tribune*, and Jean suggested to him that he write a few feature articles for the *Daily Mail*, which he did, but the editors were not interested. Jean, however, pursued the idea further by going to Pearl Adam, the wife of *The Times* Paris correspondent, George Adam, whom she had met

at a party in London during the War. After they had met a few times
Mrs Adam asked Jean if she had done any writing herself, and Jean
shyly mentioned that she had written a few slight sketches. Pearl
Adam took them and tried to make them into a fictional narrative
which she called 'Triple Sec'. [3] The project was doomed from the
beginning because Mrs Adam tended to romanticise the stories from
Jean's material, and neither was satisfied. In spite of this abortive
effort, Pearl Adam proved to be a most resourceful connection. It was
she who introduced Jean to Ford Madox Ford, who was to become
the most important literary influence in her career. Not only did Ford
work with her on her own writing, he introduced her to modern
literature, gave her reading lists, and copies of the *transatlantic review*
and other magazines which contained the best contemporary writing.
Through him, she met the prominent figures of the Paris literary
world, and although she remained at the fringes of this society, she did
meet Joyce and Hemingway. More importantly, Ford went over her
stories with her, talked to her at great length about shaping and giving
form to the subject matter. 'He knew all about writing,' Jean has
said. [4]

Although she gives Ford credit for making her into a writer, there
were a number of factors which made her a brilliant pupil and Ford an
ideal teacher. The development of Rhys's style, although guided by
Ford, was largely intuitive; it emerged out of her sense of proportion
and design, her concern for form. She attributes this intuitive quality
to a strong mathematical sense inherited from her father's side of the
family. She was not particularly good with numbers in school, but as
she reads her early drafts, she knows instinctively when something
interferes with the shape of a sentence, a paragraph, or a chapter and is
able to cut it. It is this uncanny ability from which the smooth and
polished surfaces of her work emerge, but it has also made writing
arduous for her and the final draft almost impossible to reach. She
writes draft after draft until she has created the symmetry and
wholeness which her intuitive sense of form dictates. She is also very
open about the autobiographical nature of her work: 'I always start
with something I feel or something that happened and then in the
middle it becomes something else. I add and subtract.' [5] It is through
this process that she takes the raw materials of her life and transforms
them, giving them shape and cohesion, molding them into art.

The autumn of 1924, when Jean first met Ford, was a difficult time.
She and de Nève were living from place to place much as they had
always done, and their financial problems were as acute as ever. Never

one to tell Jean just what he was doing, de Nève became even more mysterious. Evidently he got involved in the buying and selling of *objects d'art*, the ownership of which was uncertain. These activities eventually led to his arrest and imprisonment. Jean was left with no money and a child, although through the offices of Germaine Richelot, Maryvonne still had a place to stay. It was in the midst of these dire circumstances that Ford Madox Ford came into her life.

Ford was obviously impressed with Jean's potential as a writer; he had helped many other promising young writers in the past, but his interest in Jean gradually became more personal. Her plight appealed to his generous instincts, but he also became physically attracted to her. Ford at this time was living with Stella Bowen, the Australian painter, and her published reminiscences provide a one-sided and hostile but contemporary view of Jean at the time of her relationship with Ford:

Ford had fallen in love with a very pretty and gifted young woman. He had got over it in due course, but the affair had taught me many new things. It cut the fundamental tie between himself and me, and it showed me a side of life of which I had had no previous knowledge. The girl was a really tragic person. She had written an unpublishably sordid novel of great sensitiveness and persuasiveness, but her gift for prose and her personal attractiveness were not enough to ensure her any reasonable life, for on the other side of the balance were bad health, destitution, shattered nerves, an undesirable husband, lack of nationality, and a complete absence of any desire for independence. When we met her she possessed nothing but a cardboard suit-case and the astonishing manuscript. She was down to her last three francs and she was sick.

· · · ·

She took the lid off the world that she knew, and showed us an underworld of darkness and disorder, where officialdom, the bourgeoisie and the police were the eternal enemies and the fugitive the only hero. All the virtues, in her view, were summed up in 'being a sport', which meant being willing to take risks and show gallantry and share one's last crust; more attractive qualities, no doubt, than patience or honesty or fortitude. She regarded the law as the instrument of the 'haves' against the 'have nots' and was well acquainted with every rung of that long and dismal ladder by which the respectable citizen descends towards degradation.[6]

Stella Bowen's description bears the unfairness of a rival, but it does provide a firsthand account of Jean's desperate situation and the effects of her bohemian life, especially in the way it shaped her attitudes at the time she was beginning to write fiction. Once again she was desperate and dependent, once again a man came into her life, and once again it would end in bitterness. Ford's commitment to Jean was only temporary; he would soon be content to have Stella break the affair off for him.

Jean was not the first young waif whom Ford was bent on helping. More than ten years before he met Jean he picked up a girl named Gertrud Schlablowsky and, with his 'lust for rescue-work', Ford 'set aside a half hour, every night at midnight, for talk with her . . .'. Violet Hunt describes Gertrud as 'bored, pining, discontented, dying to get away, with nowhere else to go . . . wanting luxury, gaiety, new clothes . . . She called Ford Papa.' Just as Stella Bowen helped him to extricate himself from Jean, Violet Hunt saw to Gertrud's departure, 'shipping her back to Germany and eventually providing her with the money to emigrate to New South Wales'.[7] Jean's bitter entanglement with Ford became the source for her first novel, *Quartet* (1928), which will be discussed in Chapter 3.

Another view of the Ford–Rhys relationship is provided in a curious if pedestrian novel written by de Nève in 1932. In its way de Nève's book is more directly personal than *Quartet*, and, as a reflection of the actual events, seemingly more candid. Given the nature of the subject matter it is surprising that Jean helped de Nève translate *Barred* into English and that the novel is dedicated to her. The hero in *Barred* is Jan Von Leeuween and his wife is Stania. Early in the novel Jan tries to analyze his wife's actions and concludes, 'She lets herself go. She disdains consequence. She sacrifices everybody who may suffer starting with herself. But this observance of spontaneity makes everything she does seem calculated. A recklessness that is calculated can become a horrible cruelty.'[8] This 'recklessness' that de Nève saw in Jean is not far from the trait Stella Bowen observed, but it was a recklessness brought on by a haphazard and unfocused life that de Nève himself shared at the time.

More naked in its bitterness than *Quartet*, *Barred* is also much less successful as a novel. However, the book refers to a dominant element in the Rhys heroine, her passivity, as de Nève's hero speaks of this in his wife, 'I tortured myself by thinking of the strange passivity that characterised her.'[9] Leaving artistic considerations aside, these two novels mirror each other as together they detail what were probably the psychological motivations and reactions of the various people involved in this complex period in Jean's life. Both novels are too much absorbed in self-justifications. On the other hand, they are valuable to our understanding of this important part of Jean's development.

There is a kind of horrible irony in Jean Rhys's relationship with Ford. He obviously launched her career and taught her a great deal about writing fiction, but it was also his relationship with her that confirmed her deepest suspicions about her own feminine vulnerability and male exploitation. There is little doubt, as Stella Bowen records, that at the time she met Ford she had reached her lowest ebb. She was in desperate financial straits; her husband was in jail; she was unable to care for her daughter or herself as she would have liked to. She had become a creature with nowhere to go for protection, no family, no country, nowhere to return. She was entering her thirties when she met Ford, and was no longer hopeful that life would suddenly turn around. The bitter experience with Ford must have confirmed for her just how truly vulnerable women are, and how, in their desperate search for protection, they can so easily be exploited and torn apart. It was with this knowledge that she began to understand the female struggle far more acutely and was able to give a distinctive voice to the female condition. She recognised that beneath the passivity and self-destructiveness of women there was a willingness to engage in a desperate struggle for survival, just as beneath the surface ugliness of their lives there was a yearning for beauty, a new dress, an attractive room. When she at last began to pursue her literary career, Jean Rhys had both the personal experience and the understanding of her material.

When it came to her career, Ford helped her enthusiastically. He made arrangements with the American publisher, Pascal Covici, for Jean to translate Francis Carco's *Perversité*, and, in fact, became so involved in the negotiations that Covici credited Ford with the translation on the title page when the book was eventually published in 1928.

Ford also found another opportunity for Jean while de Nève was still in prison. A Mrs Huenot needed someone to help her to write a book devoted to her theories on the transmigration of species, and her particular theory had a great deal to do with recording her dreams and the acquisition of furniture from different periods so that the spirits of one's earlier lives would feel at peace. Jean saw all of this as very comic and thus enjoyed the prospects, especially the prospect of going to southern France to work on it. Mrs Huenot had grand notions of her past selves and suspected that an earlier self had held court in an eighteenth-century salon. One of her grander notions must have been fulfilled in her own life when her daughter Natoma married Rudolph Valentino.

As Jean's affair with Ford was coming to an end, her husband was finally released from prison. She wanted to meet him and go back with him, but he had suspected what Jean told him of her arrangement with Ford, and the revelation spelled the end of their marriage. Nevertheless, Jean and de Nève left Paris together and settled in Amsterdam, and Jean continued to write. She had already completed a series of stories titled *The Left Bank*, which dealt in part with the events of her early life with de Nève. In Amsterdam she was also completing the translation of Carco's *Perversité*, and de Nève helped her with the idiomatic French. Maryvonne began attending a convent school in Waerden. During these days in Amsterdam Jean and de Nève did not live as husband and wife, and both knew that the marriage had really ended. He never forgave her for becoming involved with Ford while he was in prison.

During her stay in Amsterdam Jean also completed the final draft of *Quartet*. She originally sent it to Jonathan Cape, the firm that had published *The Left Bank*, but she was told by the editors that they were afraid to publish the novel because of a possible libel action by Ford. They recognised immediately that the subject matter was too close to the actual circumstances of her life. One of the Garnetts read the book for Chatto and Windus and recommended publication, but the publisher insisted that the title be changed to *Postures*. Jean later wrote that she never really understood why Chatto insisted on changing the title. However, she agreed to the change and the novel was published in 1928.

Although neither *The Left Bank* nor *Quartet* sold very well, the reviews were encouraging. She was not terribly disappointed by the small sales, because she knew her writing would not be read with enthusiasm by a wide audience. Her work, especially *Quartet*, would seem relentlessly depressing in its portrayal of a heroine who seemed unable and even unwilling to pick herself up, change her life, make a new start—all of the things which the heroines of novels about ill-fated women were supposed to do. However well-wrought and deeply felt, her subject matter would seem narrow, confining, and even suffocating. Yet a few recognised in her work a remarkable talent.

She and de Nève finally broke off altogether, were eventually divorced, and Jean returned to England. Shortly after her arrival she met Leslie Tilden Smith, who was then a literary agent and had been a reader with several publishers including Hamish Hamilton. Her meeting with Smith was to prove extremely important for both her personal and professional life. Leslie and Jean became very close and by 1929 they began living together. They were later married and remained together until Leslie died on 2 October, 1945.

Leslie was the son of an Anglican clergyman. He came down from Merton College, Oxford in 1906 where he had read 'greats', but finished, with an added year, in geography. His interests, however, were exclusively literary and he immediately took a job with the literary agents Curtis, Brown in London. He married Kathleen Millard, a young woman who was also working at the agency, in 1909, and they had three children before World War I. Leslie served in the war, first with the Middlesex Regiment and by 1916 in France with the Royal Flying Corps. Although he and Kathleen were not divorced until the middle twenties, their marriage had really broken up during the war, especially after Kathleen had met Basil McEwan while Leslie was in France. She was later to move to India for a time after she and Basil were married. By 1929 Jean and Leslie were together in Holland Park in a flat over what had been a stable and was now a garage.

Leslie's daughter Anne would visit them periodically. Anne was twenty-one and had recently married Peter Dawson, who was in the film industry. Anne recalls her first visit during the spring of 1929, when Jean gave her a black dress which she had bought in Paris. Anne remembers sitting in the slanting light of the living room and her first sight of Jean, who was then thirty-five. Anne found her most attractive, small, slender, with large green eyes, reddish-brown hair, pale white skin, and a beautifully proportioned figure. But it was her eyes above all that were striking. Her voice was not strong and was rather high, and to Anne's ear she retained a trace of a West Indian accent.

From Boyne Terrace Mews in Holland Park, Leslie and Jean moved to 94 Elgin Crescent in 1931. During these years from 1929 to 1932, Jean made several visits back to Paris mainly to work on *After Leaving Mr Mackenzie*. With her fey gift for describing the essential impression that place makes upon her, she was recently quoted in *Time* as saying: 'Paris sort of lifted you up. It did, it did, it did! You know the light is quite pink, instead of being yellow or blue. I've never seen anything like it anywhere else.'[10]

In spite of the hard years she spent there, Paris remained at an opposite pole to London. The imagery in her fiction contrasts the two cities: London is always dark, cold, and harsh; Paris is bright and open. During the thirties she would return to Paris for short visits. She would walk through the familiar locales recalling scenes and experiences for her novels. But these trips were also an escape from England.

The years with Leslie were anything but idyllic. There were financial problems and drinking. Leslie was hopeless with money and frequently had to go to his father for help, and Jean, of course, made virtually nothing from royalties on her books. In 1934 Leslie's father died and left him £8,000, a substantial sum in the 1930s, but instead of investing the inheritance, he went through it in two years. It was about this time, too, that Jean and Leslie were married in a Registry Office in London. A portion of the inheritance was spent on a long trip to Bermuda, the West Indies, and the United States, begun in February of 1936. They spent over a month in Dominica. This was the first and only time that Jean returned to her native island. This visit was to provide her with further background for *Wide Sargasso Sea*.

In late February Jean and Leslie sailed from Southampton on *Le Cuba*, a French Line ship, for Martinique. Before settling in Dominica for an extended stay, they also visited St Lucia, where they stayed in a small hotel run by two of Jean's cousins. Lily and Monica had last seen Jean eighteen years before, when they had visited England. Leslie, in a letter to his daughter, Anne, remarked that they were greeted warmly and the cousins thought Jean looked as young as when they had seen her in England. After a brief stay in St Lucia, Jean and Leslie made the short trip to Dominica. Leslie told his daughter that they were eager to arrive so Jean could begin writing. Their object was to rent a comfortable cottage and spend at least six weeks in Dominica before returning to England by way, as it turned out, of New York and Boston. By the end of April Leslie wrote that Jean was 'working again', but 'she hasn't made much headway yet'. For Jean their stay was a return to all the scenes of her childhood, but she discovered in this return a natural discrepancy between her childhood memories of Dominica and the present reality. The mystery had been replaced by present boredom and discomfort. A week before they were to leave, Leslie wrote to his daughter:

> Jean also heard from Constable that a 2/6 edition of *Voyage in the Dark* is being put out just about now. This is very pleasing news— the first time she has been 'done cheap'. But she hasn't been very well just lately—the heat has been rather too much for her! It is getting a great deal hotter here and also much wetter.[11]

The people, their language and customs, still interested and even charmed her, but as much as anything else it was the island itself which stirred in Jean both memory and emotion. Even so, after spending so many years in Europe, the slow, languid life of Dominica now seemed to her remote and even boring. By the end of May she was anxious to leave.

Her return to her birthplace, however, was obviously important to Jean. Although she was then working on *Good Morning, Midnight*, a novel set exclusively in Paris, her next novel, *Wide Sargasso Sea*, which she would write years later, was to be set in the West Indies. This visit more than likely enabled her to integrate the experience of her childhood with a mature sensibility in order to inform the novel with the deep and complex feelings that arose within her. But her nostalgic longing for the place of her childhood had ended at last, enabling her, no doubt, to see more clearly that part of her life which had for long aroused a confusion of undefinable feelings.

As Europe drew closer to war, Jean's regular visits to the Continent were interrupted. In 1939 Maryvonne had come to England from the Netherlands, where she had been living with her father but, just before war between The Netherlands and Germany was officially declared, she returned to The Netherlands. Leslie, in the meantime, volunteered for the war; he had flown for the RFS in World War I, but he was now considered too old for active duty. He did, however, serve in various para-military capacities, and during the war he and Jean moved about England a great deal. He was stationed in Norwich and in Wales, and was sent back to London in 1944 as the V2 rockets were falling. During this period Jean spent time in London and began to write again, but she all but gave up on the prospects for success. It was more a matter of an unquenchable need to write. Leslie complained that Jean was shutting him out of her life and she agreed, because 'I don't see how you can write without shutting everything else out'.[12] And that was perhaps precisely what she was trying to do.

Leslie Smith died suddenly on 2 October, 1945. His cousin, Max Hamer, came to help Jean, and they eventually married. She records: 'I grew dependent upon him; he was rather a sweet man.'[13] Jean and Max lived in London for a number of years, but eventually moved to Cornwall and later to Devon. Her brother, Rhys Williams, told them of a place where they might be comfortable, but shortly after they moved there, Max died.

The years following the war and Leslie's death were bad times. Jean's health continued to decline, and there were serious financial problems. By 1949 she and Max were living in Beckenham, Kent. Max got into trouble over taking cheque forms from his firm, and eventually was sent to prison. Letters from Jean during this period indicate not only her intense anxiety over Max's plight, but they reveal a deep disappointment over the lack of recognition for her work. Throughout the forties and fifties, Jean remained in obscurity, trying to cope with problems of health and finances, and almost completely unable to get very far with her writing.

All of her books were, of course, out of print—she was completely forgotten as a writer. Well, not completely. Selma Vaz Dias, an actress and theatrical personality, had long admired her work and decided to adapt *Good Morning, Midnight* into a dramatic monologue to be performed on stage. She suspected that Jean Rhys was dead, since she had heard nothing of her since *Good Morning, Midnight* was published in 1939. Vaz Dias put a notice in the *New Statesman* on the off chance that if she were alive Jean would see it. Jean did see the notice and her reply began a correspondence which would span more than fifteen years.[14] Vaz Dias gave her performance at the Anglo-French Art Centre on 10 November 1949. Although this was small recognition indeed, it was of great importance to Jean; it gave her the impetus to write again after years of constant discouragement. By this time she had almost given up any hope of ever seeing her work, past or future, in print, and the fact that it had been accorded so little recognition had only deepened her sense of frustration. In spite of their eventual misunderstandings and Selma's later obsession for claiming she was the sole discoverer of Jean Rhys, the actress played an important role in bringing Rhys's career back to life.

It was nearly ten years, however, before Selma's efforts on Jean's behalf would begin to bring tangible benefit. On 10 May 1957, the BBC's Third Programme presented Selma Vaz Dias reading a radio monologue adapted from *Good Morning, Midnight* with music by Roberto Gerhard. Following the excellent reception of the performance, other, more important things began to happen. Diana Athill of Andre Deutsch was introduced to Jean's work by Francis Wyndham, a longtime and loyal admirer of her novels. It was through Selma's efforts that Jean was 'discovered' again, but Francis Wyndham, and later Diana Athill, played more important roles in actually bringing Rhys's work to public attention. But even this little attention encouraged her to begin work on a novel to be entitled *Wide Sargasso Sea*. Her recognition and success connected with the publication of *Wide Sargasso Sea* will be treated in detail in later chapters.

Even after the BBC success there were to be more years of obscurity and hardship for Jean. She had all but completed the manuscript of her new novel when she was felled by a heart attack and nearly died. After a long recovery period she finally got the manuscript to the publisher, and the publication of *Wide Sargasso Sea* brought to Jean Rhys the recognition and wide critical acclaim which had so long eluded her. Thus it was that in her seventies all of her novels were brought back into print, paperback editions were published, and increasing critical and popular recognition has continued for the past dozen years.

She now spends part of each winter in London but returns to her cottage in Cheriton Fitzpaine in the spring, where she lives alone and continues to work on her autobiography.

It is both ironic and painful that success eluded Jean Rhys until she reached her seventies. Through the medium of her novels, her moral intelligence responded to the human conditions, especially of women, that she saw and experienced herself in the twenties and thirties, but to her contemporaries, her work seemed too dark and gloomy, too unrelenting in its depiction of the exploited female victims, the fallouts of the male dominated bourgeois society. Her work, however, holds a special importance and meaning for the present. Her subtle, distinctive and radical portrayal of the female experience—a portrayal which insists on no evasions of reality—lies not only at the heart of her achievement, but also accounts in large part for the recognition that she has been accorded in this decade. The consciousness of the sixties and seventies seems better able to identify with, to understand, and to share Jean Rhys's world.

2   *The Left Bank*

Written under the tutelage of Ford Madox Ford and published with his elaborate, if not very well-focused preface, *The Left Bank*[1] is a collection of twenty-two stories and sketches which oscillate between themes and subjects of poverty, loneliness, fear of growing old, loss of beauty, displacement, women as victims of men's desires and of their own fragility and vanity. Frequently lacking in subtlety or depth, the stories nevertheless contain in embryo the themes and ideas which will dominate Rhys's novels. Too unformed to be termed an introduction to all of Rhys's subsequent work, the collection can, however, be seen as a kind of loosely structured overture to her later fiction. This analogy is suggested not merely as a critical strategy, but also because these earliest pieces, some of them no more than prose fragments really, reveal the essential attitude and sensibility toward the world underlying all her work. Already these stories and sketches show Rhys's uncanny ability to discover meaning in the selection of event or action. The reader of her novels is again and again confronted with characters in the same dire circumstances or conditions as those introduced in *The Left Bank*, but in her subsequent work we become conscious of a greater refinement of imagination and social intelligence. *The Left Bank* is a successful beginning, for, in spite of limitations, it introduces an important artist at the formative stage of her career, and we recognise from the start that this is a talented writer who is still in search of a distinctive voice but can already write gracefully and well about the grim and formless lives of her characters.

The title of this volume directs us to a distinct locale, and several of the stories are set on the Rive Gauche, but implicit in the title are matters beyond setting. As Ford Madox Ford implies in his discursive preface, 'The Left Bank' is not a topography after all, but a way of looking at life—of the 'Left Banks of the world'.[2] Ford goes on to suggest: 'I tried . . . very hard to induce the author of *The Left Bank* to introduce some sort of topography . . . in the cunning way it would have been done by Flaubert or Maupassant, or by

Mr Conrad . . . With cold deliberation . . . she eliminated even such two or three words of descriptive matter as had crept into her work . . .'(26) Obviously the author's priorities were of a different nature than Ford's, but he recognised them, for he goes on to write: 'Her business was with passion, hardship, emotions: the locality in which these things are endured is immaterial.'(26) It would be misleading, however, to eliminate Paris from our consideration, for although setting and topography are not interwoven into the narrative predominantly as background, the Paris ambience is suffused through nearly every page of the Paris stories. The descriptions which do appear are strategically developed within the narrative and psychological framework of the stories. These descriptions of Paris are, however, severely restricted and never used merely to amplify and enlarge a scene, rather the atmosphere of the city is evoked to reveal character and mood. The title extends to the thematic elements within the collection, and Paris' XIIIth Arrondissement plays a special role in many of the stories.

Paris looms so large in the life of art and literature of this century that nearly every statement about its place in modernism falls into cliché. Until she met Ford, however, Jean Rhys knew a Paris far different from that depicted in the fiction and memoirs of so many of the expatriates, especially the Americans, who found a home there. As George Wickes has pointed out:

> For these Americans Paris consisted mainly of a cluster of sidewalk cafés along the Boulevard du Montparnasse. This was a relatively new neighborhood out beyond the Latin Quarter that became the headquarters for artists and writers in the twenties. Here at the Café du Dôme, La Rotonde, or Le Select, Americans gathered to spend their days. They took readily to the café, an institution in a country where men do not usually invite friends home. Living in hotel rooms, the Americans also found it convenient to conduct their social lives in public. The cafés of Montparnasse were their clubs, where they read their American newspapers, received letters from home, and met other Americans who like themselves had little to occupy them besides an occasional trip to the Morgan Bank or American Express to cash a check. It was a pleasant way to pass one's days, and time lost its American urgency at the slow tempo of the café terrasse.[3]

This is the Paris of the 1920s that has become part of our literary

mythology of modernism and the other 'isms' of the period, but it is
not the Paris of the same period that was Jean Rhys's world, nor was it
to be the world of her heroines who scratch and struggle in its back
streets and cheap restaurants and hotels.

The districts of Montmartre and Montparnasse are the same, the
topography is the same, but Rhys's world is the underside of the
bohemian existence—the people who brought them drinks, the
whores they bedded, the dancers who cavorted before them, those
frequently pathetic background figures who gave Paris its 'local
colour', and made it seem so 'foreign' and 'alive' behind its stern
architecture.

Ford was to become Rhys's one serious personal link with the
literary world of Paris. At the time she met him he was still a central if
slightly tarnished figure in the contemporary activities of modernism.
In spite of his stature as an editor of the defunct *The English Review*
and the soon-to-die *transatlantic review*, his influence had begun to
wane amid the more recent influences of Pound, Joyce and the more
flamboyant harbingers of the new. His skirmishes with
Hemingway before the demise of the *transatlantic review*, as well as
some of the material he published in its pages, were indicative of
Ford's allegiance to an older generation. He wrote in 1927 in his
dedicatory letter to Stella Bowen for a new edition of *The Good
Soldier* of his gracious bow to a newer generation: 'Then I prepared to
stand aside in favour of our good friends—-yours and mine—Ezra,
Eliot, Wyndham Lewis, H. D. and the rest of the clamourous young
writers who were then knocking at the door'.[4] Ford was in his middle
fifties when Rhys met him, and, although his stature had declined, he
was, ironically enough, engaged in his major work, the tetralogy,
which was later to be titled *Parade's End*. He was still at the height of
his literary powers.

Whatever his personal reasons—they were no doubt
considerable—for publishing Jean Rhys's first work in *transatlantic
review* and writing the preface to her first published book, it is not
difficult to see the qualities in her writing which attracted him. Her
straightforward style, her gift for understatement and directness,
appealed to Ford's literary taste. Also, as he points out in the preface,
Rhys's work had closer affinities with French fiction than with
English, and in his preface to *The Good Soldier* he recounts what he
considers the highest praise his novel received:

I had in those days an ambition: that was to do for the English novel what in *Fort comme la mort* Maupassant had done for the French. One day I had my reward, for I happened to be in a company where a fervent young admirer exclaimed: 'By Jove, *The Good Soldier* is the finest novel in the English language!' whereupon my friend Mr. John Rodker who has always had a properly tempered admiration for my work, remarked in his clear, slow drawl: 'Ah yes. It is, but you have left out a word. It is the finest French novel in the English language!'[5]

Ford admired in Rhys's work those same qualities which he valued in his own. How much he gave or taught his willing pupil is difficult to measure, but clearly she learned and absorbed much from him. Her West Indian background, her knowledge of the French language, her strong feelings for things French, especially its contemporary literature, and her absence of a thorough knowledge of the English literary tradition combined with her considerable natural talent made her the ideal pupil for Ford. Her willingness to learn and Ford's acute literary judgment provided the combination for the emergence of her literary achievement. So, whatever was personal in their relationship, Ford's admiration for her work is significant; as Mark Schorer has pointed out, Ford's judgment of fiction '. . . was always the judgment of the craftsman'.[6] And it was precisely the craft which Rhys learned.

Underneath his somewhat overblown and cultural-topographical tour of Paris, Ford's comments about Rhys's stories provide an initial focus from which to view *The Left Bank* in a literary context. The special tone and feel of the stories seem to bear little similarity to short fiction that was being written in England at the time, and certainly the condition and fate of their heroines would have seemed exotic if not remote when compared with those of English contemporary writers. As Ford himself points out, they seem closer to the French short story before the Great War. They resemble the stories of Anatole France or Maupassant, but the resemblance is superficial, for Rhys's stories are far less polished or controlled. Hers are more Chekhovian, open-ended, than either of these two Frenchmen's. There is an echo, an air, but nothing substantial. In some ways the best ones resemble Katherine Mansfield's stories, but the settings, the characters, the social world, all are very different. They are closest to the stories of Colette. But although they deal with sexual relationships and exploitation, they are devoid of Colette's sensuality; Rhys's women are far less spirited, more resigned. And if the motive point in

Colette's fiction is freedom, Rhys's stories point in the opposite direction. Like Colette, however, whom she admires as much as any woman writer, she shies away from abstraction. As Germaine Bree has observed of Colette, 'she developed a personal perspective in the long meditations that sustained her relation with what she observed'.[7] This quality in Colette's art is also apparent in Rhys's fiction, but the measure of direct influence is difficult to gauge, complicated by the deeply personal nature of Rhys's art. Rhys's work possesses a certain affinity with many of the attitudes found in Colette's fiction, the knowing awareness of women and their motivations, the compression, the subtlety. On the other hand, Colette's world is far broader and possesses a wider range of treatment. One recognises this affinity, but to argue for direct influence is far more difficult. What these stories do share with Colette's and Mansfield's, to a lesser extent, is obvious, though no small achievement: the creation of an entirely feminine world—a world where the ordering and interpretation are exclusively feminine, and a world where the feminine consciousness is not seen in the reflection of a masculine universe.

Although there were no clear models or visible influences on this early collection, its traditional style and the essential clarity of her work occasioned attentive notices. The review in *TLS* noted that her '. . . sketches and short character studies seem almost tentative'.[8] *The New York Times* review got closer to the characteristics of her work, describing her method as a rejection of the descriptive, expository, and structured plot, but noted that hers is a '. . . gift of connotation, to grasp in a moment all that is behind the situation and inherent in the character'.[9] The reviewer goes on to suggest a vague similarity to Katherine Mansfield's work. Perhaps the most perceptive notice appeared in the *Saturday Review*, where the reviewer concluded that '. . . the book as a whole indicates that Rhys's vision of things has not yet clarified, though the tricks of her trade are already mastered'.[10]

The reviewers above are essentially accurate in their observations, for beyond the tentative and fragmentary nature of many of the individual stories, there is no centrality of focus to the volume as a whole—there is not yet a distinctive voice pervading the work. For example, Paris was later to play an important role in her fiction; the evocation of Paris became a means by which her themes would be carried forward. But even the title in this volume seems to have been in response to Ford's introduction rather than one which embraced the whole work; the longest and best work, for example, is largely set in and titled 'Vienne'. Unity, in short, is not achieved through place in all of its aspects as it is in Joyce's *Dubliners*, where the city emerges as a central and dynamic force and its influence is seen in nearly all the characters' fates. For Joyce the city modulates and unifies his artistic vision of the microcosm, and Dublin becomes a world intricately related to the themes of all the stories and the complex fate of the characters who live there. The so-called plotlessness of *Dubliners* is diminished by the reflexive quality of each story upon the others and upon the whole. Rhys's collection, like *Dubliners*, relies on the concrete, but it is not naturalistic, nor is it accretive; therefore the sketches remain incomplete and the whole does not become greater than the sum of its parts; the quality of each story or sketch rests on its own merit or weakness, for the book's effect, unlike that of *Dubliners*, which forms an integrated whole without losing the individual integrity of each story, is not cumulative. Topography had not yet become an integrated element in her fiction.

The Left Bank does offer, however, more than a view of Rhys's apprenticeship: it introduces the major themes which were to preoccupy her mature work, and it establishes many of the essential attitudes of her characters. Most important, and perhaps this is in retrospect, we see the development of the craft that will carry us into her imaginative world.

The first story, 'Illusion', one of the nine stories from *The Left Bank* which Rhys included in her volume, *Tigers are Better Looking* (1968), is simple and even rudimentary in design; yet there is a controlled focus, a sharpness of detail, and a splendid ending which compensate for the intrusive strokes of the narrator. The story is structured around one of the most obvious devices of the genre, the inevitable reversal of appearances. The self-imposed limitations, the objectivity of observations, and the unfailing directness create proportion and balance.

The narrator describes her acquaintance, Miss Bruce, a mediocre English painter ('just clever enough and not too clever' 29), who seems completely untouched by the life she observes in the Quarter. The second paragraph sets up the movement of the entire story:

> She was a tall, thin woman, with large bones and hands and feet. One thought of her as a shining example of what character and training—British character and training—can do. After seven years in Paris she appeared utterly untouched, utterly unaffected, by anything hectic, slightly exotic or unwholesome. Going on all the time all round her were the cult of beauty and the worship of

physical love: she just looked at her surroundings in her healthy, sensible way, and then dismissed them from her thoughts . . . rather like some sturdy rock with impotent blue waves washing round it. (29)

'Appeared' is the operative word, for Miss Bruce, with her conservative English ways, seems far removed from the gaudy, glamourous but manic life of the women of Paris who are probably the subjects of her portraits. This contrast is described almost too obviously by the narrator, though she cautions us that ' . . . I only know the outside of Miss Bruce—the cool, sensible, tidy English outside.'(31)

The inevitable revelation of the darker side of Miss Bruce, and the 'illusion' she has created, presents itself to the narrator when she comes to her apartment, is greeted by the concierge and told Miss Bruce has been taken ill so quickly that she did not have time to pack, so the narrator goes to her room to gather several gowns and essentials. She finds in the wardrobe colourful clothes of the choicest designs, perfumes and cosmetics of all descriptions. The cold, objective Miss Bruce who appeared to look at the foibles of her sex with such disdain, is a closet 'petite femme', subject to all the vanities of her sisterhood but too afraid to reveal herself—forced by her hidden vanity to create the illusion of distance and superiority.

But the essence of the story lies deeper than the narrator's discovery. The story's achievement is realised on the final page when two or three weeks later Miss Bruce and the narrator dine together and Miss Bruce says, 'I should never make such a fool of myself as to wear them. . . . They ought to be worn, I suppose.'(36) But just then:

A plump, dark girl, near us, gazed into the eyes of her dark, plump escort, and lit a cigarette with the slightly affected movements of the non-smoker.

'Not bad hands and arms, that girl!' said Miss Bruce in her gentlemanly manner.(36)

It is in this closing passage that the title, theme, and central focus are amply rendered. The subtle and almost imperceptible shift in focus from the narrator's observations and insights to those of Miss Bruce herself gives added dimension to what would otherwise be a rather obvious observation, for it provides an additional perspective on the nature of defence and timidity.

A number of the pieces in the collection are carefully drawn sketches which reveal the hidden emotions of the figures populating 'Tout Montparnasse'. In many of these there is a victim who absorbs human cruelty with little or no capacity for defence. In 'A Spiritualist', for example, the Commandant narrates a cold, depressing little tale in much the same manner as the Duke in Browning's 'To My Last Duchess', but without the Duke's knowing irony. The Commandant's woeful ignorance of his former mistress's plight is, in fact, the point of the story. As Rhys's later fiction reveals, the deck is so stacked against these victims that the dealers are oblivious to any other possible outcome. The Commandant begins his tale with the declaration: 'I assure you . . . that I adore women—that without a woman in my life I cannot exist.'(37) In his mean tale, as with many of the other stories, both perpetrator and victim are unaware that they could have behaved in any other way.

Women are not the sole victims, for sexual exploitation is only a major symptom of a far more pervasive disease. 'From a French Prison', a slightly overdrawn story of a jailer (the holder of society's keys), the incarcerated victims, and their visitors, presents a picture of people unable to comprehend the world of law and bourgeois legislation. An old man and a boy come to the jail on visiting day. The old man's cataracts blind him, and his inability to understand the language reveals the larger failure of society's victims to comprehend the elaborate protections which one part of humanity devises to separate itself from the other. When asked for his visiting card, the old man's eyes fill with tears thinking it will be taken away from him, and the jailer delights in his anxiety. Two girls, probably prostitutes, explain the procedure to him. The girls remain in touch with both worlds, for they live by their wits and others' lusts, and this requires their keeping a knowing eye on both worlds. It is not just the aged who are victims, for at the close of the story the little boy's 'mouth drooped, his huge brown eyes stared solemnly at an incomprehensible world'.(47) In this story Rhys is too dependent on her ability to imply with little exposition the full emotional impact of an experience, for the story lacks dramatic motive power for the pathos depicted at its close. A failure of this kind is rare in her work, for understatement and detachment become two of the most significant qualities in her novels.

It has been observed that *The Left Bank* does not have an integrated pattern upon which even the sketches could achieve a balance within the entire framework of the collection, nor, in the broadest sense, does topography function as a structuring device. But this is not to say that there is no organisational impulse within the collection. For example, 'Trio' is a brief observation of three Caribbeans in a Montparnasse restaurant. Their uninhibited and sensual behaviour recalls for the narrator her own childhood spent in the Antilles. This sketch forms an introduction to the next two stories, 'Mixing Cocktails' (one of the best in the collection) and 'Again the Antilles', which are set in exotic Dominica. The world depicted in this setting is viewed with fond recollection, but nostalgia does not obscure the narrator's sharpness or insight. In depicting life in this 'wild place' where 'everything was still and languid, worshipping the sun'(89) there is an implicit contrast made with the atmosphere and topography of the Rive Gauche; indeed, these sketches reflect more on the present than on the past, a subtle rendering of past experience to bring the present into sharper focus. 'Mixing Cocktails' describes a young girl's vague awakening into the adult world amid the contrast of a British Colonial upbringing and the lush, sensuous world of Dominica. Every evening she serves up the mix of angostura, limes, and gin, measuring it out with 'uncanny intuition' for the colonial cocktail hour. But this ritual in no way dims her awareness of the exotic world which surrounds her, where 'the moon does bad things to you if it shines on you when you sleep'.(91) Both the incidents and atmosphere from this story recur in *Voyage in the Dark*.

'Again the Antilles' is a vignette about an exchange in the newspaper between an English landowner and the 'coloured' editor of the *Dominica Herald and Leeward Islands Gazette*, which offers a humourous insight into the racial attitudes of them both. Together these three sketches present the imaginative inception of West Indian material which will be integrated into her later work, reaching its fullest development in *Wide Sargasso Sea*. As her novels draw closer and closer to a precise and complex rendering of her own experience, her treatment of the West Indian background will play a curious and complicated role in her imaginative depiction of its relationship to her heroines, but in these stories it remains distant.

The more intense stories in the volume are more occupied with the present; for example, 'Hunger' is a raw and naked sketch, told in the first person, of a young woman who describes her feelings—both physical and psychological—as she lies in her hotel room without money to afford food. For five days she has had only coffee; she eats bread at midday, but she has been doing that for a long time and it no longer seems worth the effort. The acceptance of her condition and the ironic rendering of her fate with its understated and flat descriptions ('it is a frankly awful business') anticipate in an embryonic way the characteristics and attitudes of the female character which is to be developed in later novels. In 'Hunger', however, the psychological numbness and underlying frustrations, while told from the intimacy of the first person, are not effectively achieved. The motives which lie behind the narrator's tale are absent, making dramatic realisation of her plight impossible. Important for our consideration, however, is the fact that we see here emerging a fatalistic attitude toward the inevitable helplessness of women—a post-Darwinian acceptance of human inequality and the impossibility of confronting those forces which seem predisposed to annihilate the weak, however fiercely they struggle. This process of selection and rejection in human and social terms is seen through power-plays involving sex and money. Women are the inevitable casualties, as the narrator in 'Hunger' points out:

Lying in bed, my arm over my eyes, I despise, utterly, my futile struggles of the last two years. What on earth have I been making such a fuss about? What does it matter, anyway? Women are always ridiculous when they struggle.

It is like being suspended over a precipice. You cling for dear life with people walking on your fingers. Women do not only walk: they stamp.

Primitive beings, most women.(100–1)

This passage is especially revealing, for it anticipates what is to emerge as a fundamental attitude of the Rhys heroine who struggles against what she knows to be an impossible set of circumstances. This knowledge, however, fails to destroy the heroine's vanity, her search for protection, her desire somehow to continue; in fact, this is consistent with Rhys's view of the world, where the weak are drawn to the strong, however destructive the attraction proves to be.

My overriding reaction to 'Hunger', however, is dissatisfaction—despite the quiet and confident tone of the narrator there is an element of sensationalism and melodrama. We are not offered a sufficient cause for the emotional dilemma that the narrator presents to us—a dilemma not whether to starve or not, but to work as a mannequin, or do something else to acquire 'means'. The narrator's only comment is that she is doomed, and yet we are not given an explanation as to why her talents, which seem to allow her to at least engage in the struggle, are not used. If use of these talents generates merely occasions for further exploitation and defeat, it is not made apparent. In its curious way the story raises a number of lingering questions, admittedly not fully formed, which Rhys was to handle artistically in her novels in any number of ways, but which here remain incomplete philosophically. Or perhaps they lie buried beneath the desires and motivations of the characters as part of the mystery which compels some to go on and others to stop, or at most allow themselves to be completely propelled by those forces which seem inevitably to operate on them. It is somewhere in this dilemma where all of Rhys's women find themselves, and if we as readers of her fictions fail to find or be comforted by a strength within these victims that enables them to triumph over their miserable condition, we are rewarded by a remarkable perception of their struggle for at least survival against this process of selection. It is difficult to create empathetic characters within such limitations without turning a story into something merely maudlin and melodramatic, as 'Hunger'. But we have in this story the formation of an essential attitude toward life that Rhys will later convey with such delicacy and careful narrative control and focus that the female figure achieves stature.

Rhys's creative energy is in itself a force against the world which her art depicts. The dislocating and disturbing impulses, the absence of moral order, the failure of the will except for mere survival, these conditions become sources of energy for her art, for rather than repress them she confronts the dark image of life they impose.

'La Gross Fifi' reflects the same darkness as 'Hunger', but, more subtly rendered and fully developed, it explores the pathetic struggle to survive against those elements which destroy us. Man's inevitable destruction is preordained, and Rhys's embodiment of this vision comes to be the figure of the woman exploited and victimised by men, her physical beauty ravaged by time and by the alcohol and pills which numb the pain of struggle, and the ironic hopelessness of her dependent condition in the face of natural forces, both social and biological, which eventually destroy her.

During a bad time toward the end of her affair with Ford, Rhys spent a short time in Nice. Her stay there provides the material for 'La Gross Fifi', which is the penultimate story in *The Left Bank* and the most sustained narrative in the collection. Wisely, she uses her own experience and depression in a subsidiary role to concentrate her focus on an aging prostitute who is stabbed in the throat and murdered by her gigolo lover. The young woman who narrates the story is named Roseau (a suggestion of her West Indian background). Roseau has been staying at the same cheap hotel as Fifi; she is attempting to recover from a broken love affair. Fifi, in her flamboyant and worldly-wise way comforts Roseau and she immediately responds, feeling that 'Fifi was as kind as God'.(175) Fifi offers Roseau advice, telling her to find a man, 'a chic type'. Her advice, however, is ominous: 'Yes, that is life—one nail drives out the other nail.'(177) But Fifi's own painful experiences with men are even more revealing, as Roseau later observes, ' . . . her gigolo turned the screw'.(181) And the metaphor becomes literally appropriate as he finally thrusts the knife.

Having adopted a narrative of Fifi's experiences rendered through Roseau, who is only beginning to endure what seems to be the long series of disastrous relationships with men, Rhys ties Roseau and Fifi through a series of identifications. Fifi is Roseau's doppelganger, and the power of the story resides in Roseau's implicit recognition that her life is somehow anticipated by Fifi, for their souls possess similar shapes. By the end of the story it is apparent that Roseau will see life through the same lens as Fifi; she sees in herself the same careless romantic spirit that will continually look for another nail to replace the pain of the last one. For Fifi naïve hope replaces sentiment; somehow it blocks out the past and makes life durable. This attitude, while ultimately destructive, helps to expiate the pain. Much of Rhys's later work will dramatise the human costs and consolations of such an attitude. How much life is possible within this outlook? How much can be mediated by it? What, if anything, can be done to escape from the pathos of its result? These questions are repeated again and again by the reader as he experiences Rhys's texts. Her artistic self engages us in their exploration of the ways in which we doom ourselves in the irrational attempt to find a living current in the desolation of life, even if the current always leads in the end to disillusionment and destruction. Rhys's fictions become intensely expressive of the cruel fate that life deals her characters, and 'La Gross Fifi' looks forward in a fundamental way to the circumstances and situations which will draw so many of her themes to our experience. This essentially negative vision provides a crux for understanding so many dimensions of the human motivation and conflict which her themes treat.

'Vienne', the last and longest story in the collection, is at once an

autobiographical saga of the restless and heady days of the reconstruction period in Middle-Europe after World War I, and a kind of
meditation on the formation of a consciousness as it responds to the
chaotic life of these cities and the period itself. A series of
kaleidoscopic sketches which run from winter 1920–1 through the
following summer trace the gaiety against a background of cor-
ruption and avarice, the good times against a haunting sense of
foreboding on the part of the narrator, and, finally, the escape from
the chaos and its authorities. 'Vienne' tells the story of Francine and
Pierre, a young couple who come to Vienna. Pierre works for the
Japanese representatives of the Allied Commission and profits by
manipulations and other shady practices on the monetary exchange.
He is finally caught out in Budapest, and the couple flee temporarily
to Prague. The story ends with Francine wanting to go back to
London, but Pierre insisting that they go to Warsaw.

The story's angle of vision is rendered exclusively through
Francine, and as she interprets these rapidly shifting scenes the reader
becomes aware of two levels of narration, the first devoted to
Francine's interpretation of the external scene, the people, the cities,
the flux of life in these post-war capitals; underneath this level of
narration, however, lies another current—the development of a
personal and deeper revelation of the experience for Francine, and it is
here where the power of the story lies.

The opening scenes focus on the café life of Vienna, once peopled
by the old aristocracy, but now filled with Western Europeans and
Japanese, the victors. The only losers present are the pretty young
girls who become their partners. There are Lysyl, Tillie, Ridi, and
many others. They are hard and yet vulnerable; of Ridi, Francine
says: 'I couldn't have hurt her if I'd been a man, too defenseless, too
easy to smash, but few men care a damn about that—or women
either.'(200) Their friend André is taken for everything by one of the
girls, and Francine observes, '"Eat or be eaten" is the inexorable law
of life. The next girl perhaps—will be sweet and gentle. His turn to be
eater. Destestable world.'(208) But during these early days there is so
much wine, so many good times that Francine reflects only briefly on
this callous and bitter underside of the experience. Pierre becomes
successful at the exchange, and Francine lives on the crest of the wave:
'Good to have money, money. All the flowers I wanted. All the
compliments I wanted. Everything, everything.'(221) It is in this
mood she pronounces an invocation to money:

Oh, great god money—you make possible all that's nice in life.
Youth and beauty, the envy of women, and the love of men.

Even the luxury of a soul, a character and thoughts of one's own
you give, and only you. To look in the glass and think I've got
what I wanted.

I gambled when I married and I've won.

As a matter of fact I wasn't so exalted really, but it was
exceedingly pleasant.

Spending and spending. And there was always more.(222)

But amid the gaiety and extravagance Francine's basic pessimism
intrudes: 'One day I had a presentiment.'(222) She asks Pierre how
much money they really have, for she knows that money is more than
a ticket to pleasure; it is the one thing that protects you, insulates you
from the situation ' . . . where every second-rate fool can have their
cheap little triumph over you—judge you with their middle-class
judgment'.(225) Her instincts tell her that they must flee: 'Clear off—
Different life, different people. Go to England—Be quite different.'(230) Her 'angel' exhorts her to pack her trunk and leave, that
dangers of all kinds lurk, but the 'Poor angel . . . you hadn't a chance
in that lovely night of Vienne.'(230) Pierre only provokes her anxiety
when he tells her they must go to Budapest. It is there that she
discovers she is pregnant, 'plunged in a placid dream of ma-
ternity'.(235) This discovery, however, is immediately followed by
Pierre's revelation that the authorities are after him; he thinks of
killing himself, but Francine exhorts him to escape and they flee to
Prague, knowing that they must quickly leave there. Their entire
flight is set against the background of the chaotic political and social
turmoil that goes on in each of these capitals. They are caught up in
their own webs but, as Francine suspected from the beginning, the
larger webs have captured them too.

The episodic structure of this story, together with its historic
background of post-war helter-skelter life, is remarkably suited to so
many of the themes and attitudes which emerge. The deeper personal
reality is embodied in Francine's fears and cynical view of life, and this
becomes increasingly more evident as the larger events begin to act on
her and Pierre; they confirm not only her fears and qualms, but verify
for her, at least, her essential attitude toward life. Her misogyny—
'Lord, how I hate most women here, their false smiles, their ferocious
jealousies of each other, their cunning—like animals'(231)—leads her
to compare her fellow creatures to animals, to a vision of the world

where, despite its moments of relief, human beings survive by preying on the weak, and even the weak are made ugly by the defences they prepare. Helplessness carries no redeeming grace; it only brings out further cruelty and stupidity on the part of the weak. 'Vienne' is an important story, for we see in the development of Francine's underlying attitudes a harbinger of the more fully developed heroine of Rhys's later novels. The motive force becomes more complex as the failing heroines combat adversity and develop an almost perverse and certainly mysterious instinct for survival going beyond those natural laws of selection which seem to determine their fates.

The Left Bank is an interesting reconstruction of experience containing a number of sharp observations, well-focused incidents, and clearly rendered situations. Although some of the sketches and stories lack a centrality of focus, a sureness and precision of treatment, a number of them are quite effective. They reflect Rhys's initial struggle to wed subject matter and experience to artistic vision and theme. They reveal the struggle of an author seeking her identity, probing for subject and style, trying to lift personal experience to art. It is in this last struggle that many of the stories fail, but in her attempt to objectify experience, we see the central direction that her later fiction will take.

3 Quartet

The sketches in *The Left Bank and Other Stories* represented an apprenticeship completed and an initial impulse fulfilled. The author had learned from Ford Madox Ford the idiom in which modern fiction was to be rendered effectively, and how personal experience could be transmuted into the subject matter of art. Her intuitive sense of form gave several of these short stories originality, centrality of focus, and unity of theme. The novel, however, creates enlarged and different demands; it is a genre more complex, more sustained and, if it permits less refinement, it also calls for a more substantial rendering of character and a more amplified definition of experience.

Written and published during the height of literary modernism, *Quartet* (1928) had much to commend it as a product of the modernist movement—its sparse style, the author's gift for understatement and irony, the careful rendering of the heroine's preoccupations in a hostile, alienating urban environment. But central to modernist art is the concept, best exemplified in English by Joyce and Eliot, of the impersonality of the artist, the notion that the artist was to be refined out of the work of art: an art so impersonal that the subject might well follow the contours of the autobiographical self such as Joyce's Stephen Dedalus, but the artist himself remains beyond his handiwork, refined out of existence. For the modernist this concept was neither sleight of hand nor sophistry; it entailed a conscious artistry, a predilection for the formal properties and organic elements of art, a deep commitment to the allusive, the mythic, and a subordination of the traditional narrative concerns of the realistic novel such as plot, event, and resolution of the characters' circumstances.

Rhys's art shares many of these characteristics and impulses of literary modernism, but she was unaware of or removed from many of its preoccupations. Like Virginia Woolf, she had to resolve for herself special problems of authorial control. In her first novel she may occasionally appear to hover too closely over her heroine's misfortunes to achieve complete aesthetic detachment. But her scrupulously disciplined style, and adroit rendering of consciousness through imagery and metaphor, expand the dimensions of the novel. In short, she creates a form suitable for this close relationship between the self and a fully realised character. Although her later novels reveal greater aesthetic control and authorial distance, her work was never very closely attuned to the technical innovations of modernism; her art developed out of an intensely private world—a world whose sources of inspiration were neither literary nor intellectual.

Her acquaintance with the modern writers was relatively slight; most of her reading immediately prior to her writing career was in late nineteenth and early twentieth-century French literature. Ford Madox Ford recognised Rhys's distinctive qualities from the beginning when he pointed out her particular preoccupations and influences in his preface to *The Left Bank*. He noted that her literary affinities were not with her contemporaries, but rather with writers such as Anatole France, and he could have added Colette.

Rhys's relationship to the widely varied currents of modernism is difficult to untangle because of her unusual background and the circumstances which brought her to write in the first place. But one important element which she shared with so many writers of her generation was the problem of moral ambiguity. From the beginning of her writing career her work assumed the modifications necessary in describing human motivation and will after Freud. This is in no way to suggest that Rhys was a conscious Freudian, or even that she knew anything about Freud in a formal sense, but rather that her work reflects the modern relativism that had come into being and was central to the shaping forces of modernist literature. Her heroines thus live in a world not shaped by a clear code of social or moral behaviour delineating which actions are 'good' and which are 'bad'. Rhys never probed the unconscious as Virginia Woolf or Marcel Proust did, but the world she created is obviously post-Freudian in its treatment of character, arrangement of consciousness, and development of theme. And this intuitive understanding contributed to the modernist character of her work.

The importance of *Quartet* in the Rhys canon is difficult to over-emphasise, for it reveals the discovery and initial development of that original voice and tone which was to characterise and define her fiction throughout the 1930s. Although we find little of the heightened sense of irony and biting wit of the later novels in *Quartet*, it does record the beginning of what was to become Rhys's distinctive style. In spite of certain flaws and limitations, *Quartet* initiates most of the major themes preoccupying Rhys's later fiction. The technical problems, overcome in her later work, also provide clues to the way in which she achieved her later technical mastery. Equally important, *Quartet* also introduces the paradigmatic Rhys heroine, a figure who with only slight transmutation will appear in all her fiction of the 1930s. Julia Martin of *After Leaving Mr Mackenzie* (1931), Anna Morgan of *Voyage in the Dark* (1934), Sasha Jansen of *Good Morning, Midnight* (1939), all exhibit at various stages of development the general characteristics and attitudes of the heroine in *Quartet*. Although each is a fully drawn and well defined character in her own right, collectively they form a stark portrait of the feminine condition in the modern world. Even though these women, because of their similar backgrounds, represent only a segment of women in the world, the depth of their plights and the nature of their struggles reveal many of the broad social and moral issues against which the feminine consciousness must contend. The heroine of *Quartet* is the first figure who goes into the make-up of this sad and woeful portrait of denigration and abuse.

Whatever its limitations, *Quartet* signalled the emergence of a distinctive voice in English fiction. Besides creating a heroine totally innocent of bourgeois values and institutions, Rhys introduced a style—to be perfected and further refined in her later novels—which was admirably suited to the preoccupations of the heroine, and the subtle revelation of her nature. Hers is a style which not only reinforces the pressing themes of her novels, but also discovers and manifests the themes as it reveals the underlying attitude of the narrative voice toward the heroine, which lies within that surface brittleness of the style itself. As readers, we become increasingly conscious of the nature of her characters, not merely through action, motivation, or exertion of the will on their part, but also through the rendering of their respective consciousnesses in a style always insightful and revealing. Carefully modulated, terse, frequently flat, always understated, the style penetrates surface situations to probe deeply into the underlying relationships and conditions of the characters.

The heroine of *Quartet* is a young woman, Marya, who has married Stephan Zelli, a young Pole who traffics in stolen art works. 'On a June afternoon, heavy with heat, they arrived in Paris'[1] from London and have been there four years, except for a long stay in Brussels. Even though Stephan is 'secretive' and a 'liar' he is 'a gentle and expert lover'. In spite of their precarious life together, she is happy, for as the narrator tells us: 'Marya, you must understand, had not been suddenly and ruthlessly transplanted from solid comfort to the hazards of Montmartre . . . . Truth to say, she was used to a lack of solidity and of fixed backgrounds.'(15) She was '. . . reckless, lazy, a vagabond by nature . . . '.(14) From the opening chapters the rather vague and aimless nature of Marya's character is established; it is suggested that her early disillusionment in trying to become an actress and ending up in a chorus line has made her passive; 'she began to live her hard and monotonous life very mechanically and listlessly'.(16) Her passivity explains a great many of Marya's attitudes and reactions and characterises her personality throughout the novel as she becomes entrapped in a number of situations which she has more or less drifted into rather than decisively chosen. The narrator stresses Marya's passive nature from the beginning, because, among other things, it explains her curious attachment to her husband and, later, her lover. More importantly, it is the exploration of this 'passivity' which lies at the heart of the novel.

When Stephan is finally arrested and sent to prison for one year, Marya is left with no money and must once again fend for herself, a prospect for which she is hardly fit. As she passes through the Paris streets, her walk characterises her condition: 'She spent the foggy day in endless, aimless walking . . . [to] escape the fear that hunted her'.(33) Her vulnerability is driven home to her and the world is once again harsh and naked, as she senses it always was:

> It was a vague and shadowy fear of something cruel and stupid that had caught her and would never let her go. She had always known that it was there—hidden under the more or less pleasant surface of things. Always. Ever since she was a child.(33)

In spite of her fears, she urges herself '. . . to have some guts', but from the beginning we are aware that she is incapable of facing the world without protection. Her premonition in the passage above foreshadows the 'cruel' and 'stupid' forces which will entrap her.

Protection is offered very quickly, however. A couple whom Marya has met, H. J. and Lois Heidler, suggest she move into a spare bedroom in their flat. The Heidlers live near the centre of the expatriate, bohemian life of Paris; she paints in a dilatory way, and he is an art dealer who champions young painters. These are the 'good Samaritans' of the epigraph toward which the bitterness of the novel is pointed:

. . . Beware
Of good Samaritans—walk to the right
Or hide thee by the roadside out of sight
Or greet them with the smile that villains wear.
R. C. Dunning

The admonishment in the epigraph, however, is curious, for the weight of the novel is certainly directed to the last line; Marya, unable to hide, is also unable to fix the right smile, or assume the appropriate posture. It is through the perception of this conundrum that the original title of the novel, *Postures*, might have come to mind, but the later title, *Quartet*, the one which Rhys preferred, suggests a broader scope to the overall theme, and places a more proper emphasis on the complexity of relationships between the Heidlers, Marya and Stephan. Furthermore, to prepare a pose is beyond Marya's scope; she is a creature without guile—her sense of self-preservation grows out of aimlessness. It is not in her nature to assume postures requiring decisiveness and direction. However, this is not to suggest that Marya is fundamentally an honest victim unable to recognise what moral issues may be involved. Morality is not an issue with her. She is vulnerable but she is not a victim of her own moral code of behaviour. Survival and protection are the motivating forces behind her actions, allowing her to fool herself for a while.

Her helpless situation inevitably draws her to the Heidlers; Marya's need for comfort and any kind of reassurance leads her to create the illusion that Heidler is a strong security figure: 'He was a rock of a man with his big shoulders and his quiet voice.'(43) Yet, her instincts are nearly always acute; when she first meets Heidler, before Stephan's incarceration, she sees in his eyes 'a curious underlying expression of obtuseness—even of brutality'.(11) The centre of her restricted world, however, moves closer and closer to the Heidlers; although she professes her love for Stephan when she visits him in prison, she does so 'hopelessly', 'for she felt that he was withdrawn from her, enclosed in the circle of his own pain, unreachable'.(45) The complexities of this potential relationship with the Heidlers are dismissed without a great deal of concern, for, although the prospect fills her with 'extraordinary dismay', she thinks: 'After all . . . it might be fun.'(49) Since she has lost one protector temporarily, and needs another, she allows herself to drift or be taken in without weighing the possible consequences.

Actually, it is Lois Heidler who convinces Marya that she should live with them, by pointing out the limited alternatives for a young woman without money. The prospects are, of course, bleak, and this is an important aspect of the entire novel—a subject to be discussed in detail later. Lois, in a sense, has seduced her, but with so few options Marya is willing. The Heidlers attribute higher motives to themselves and are initially half-convinced that they want to protect Marya, but the real truth is they want Marya as a bed companion for Heidler— Lois to keep him from straying permanently, moved by some romantic gesture in his lust, and Heidler himself, not so much to protect Marya, but to feel the warmth of her small and supple body next to him. From the beginning, then, the motives of both the Heidlers are clear, whatever surfaces they present to Marya and whatever credit for benign intentions they extend to themselves.

Chapter Seven is a deceptively simple transitional chapter, but what it does is complete the prior phase of her life with Stephan and prepare for the inevitable move to the Heidlers. It forms the necessary psychological bridge for Marya. Stephan's insistence that she live with her own 'country-people' provides the final impetus for the move; more importantly, he also offers some implicit moral justification which is really what she wants, for her financial situation is such that her options are futile ones anyway. Through a clever manipulation of the situation she has forced Stephan to insist she go, and then agrees to do so 'to quieten him and make him happier'.(57) Having elicited this response, however, she still moves to the Heidlers with a 'sense of the futility of all things'.(57) This kind of action may seem to belie my point that Marya is not calculating, but I would contend that she is not concerned with 'good' or 'bad' or guilt, but rather with survival.

There is in Marya a sense of a lost past which has been stolen from her, and it is this sense of loss and being plunged into a fearful and 'shallow world' that allows her to move from one circumstance to another finding protection from the shadows. The unalterable separation from her past is made abundantly clear in the postscript of a letter from her aunt, from whom Marya has requested money: 'Have you thought of visiting the British clergyman resident in Paris? He might be able to help you.'(58) This suggestion also recalls her past, but the force of the six earlier chapters renders the full irony which points up the inseparable gulf experience has hollowed out between Marya's past and present. Walking back to the train from the prison, Marya stood for a long time watching a little girl on a merry-go-round, and this picture '. . . made her feel more normal, less like a grey ghost walking in a vague, shadowy world'.(57)

Marya's early days with the Heidlers are very deftly drawn and developed through a carefully selected pastiche of scenes which illustrate not only her increasing reliance on the Heidlers but the way in which their world gradually becomes a large part of hers. Lois's long monologues gradually drive a wedge between the two women; Marya continues to admire her benefactress during these early days, but the initial 'soft intimacy' quickly fades. Lois is also frequently the object of the narrator's irony: 'Lois also discussed Love, Childbirth (especially childbirth, for the subject fascinated her), Complexes, Paris, Men, Prostitution, and Sensitiveness, which she thought an unmitigated nuisance.'(61) Far more devastating, however, are Marya's own reflections on Lois and their relationship: ' "Lois is as hard as nails," she would find herself thinking. A sentence she had read somewhere floats fantastically into her mind: " 'It's so nice to think that the little thing enjoys it too,' said the lady, watching her cat playing with a mouse." '(62)

In spite of her growing difficulties with Lois, the world of the Heidlers is for Marya a glittering one. At the same time, the chic, intelligent, but seemingly unreal world frightens her and inexorably she is drawn to Heidler. At this stage their relationship is undefined, 'but when they danced together she felt a definite sensation of warmth and pleasure'.(63) As the days wear on she and Heidler are inevitably drawn together; even before any words are exchanged or any strongly conscious sexual feeling emerges, her senses anticipate the ambivalence of the relationship: 'There was a smell of spring in the air. She felt unhappy, excited, strangely expectant.'(65) Heidler himself is at first enigmatic and shy, unable to approach Marya. Once again it is necessary for Lois to pave the way for Heidler's advances. In an awkward, rude, and callow manner Heidler tells Marya that he has wanted her from the first time he saw her, and goes on to say in his inimitable charming way that '. . . I know that somebody else will get you if I don't. You're that sort.'(72) In spite of their initial row, as they walked out of the café together, he took her arm in his, and 'when he touched her she felt warm and secure, then weak and so desolate that tears came into her eyes'.(73) This instant flow of mixed emotion depicts clearly Marya's dilemma; she is drawn to Heidler by her need for protection and security, but at the same time she must attempt to reconcile this need with her obligations to the other two members of the 'Quartet', Stephan and Lois.

Stephan is so wrapped up in his own self-torture that he seems to have pulled away from any concern with Marya. Lois, fearful that Heidler could run off with Marya and aware that his hot lust for her will gradually dissipate, if he can realise his lust while they are under the same roof, encourages Marya to remain in the household as Heidler's lover—the *ménage à trois* begins with a variety of mixed motives and compromises. Marya's compromise has to do with a certain abandonment of her will; she looks upon her dilemma not so much in moral terms, for she has released herself from that by seeing herself as 'a victim'. She recalls what a sculptor once told her: 'Victims are necessary so that the strong may exercise their will and become more strong.'(73) She inverts the Nietzschean cry for self-justification of the strong by applying it to the weak, but having arrived at this position, she still feels the strong urge to retreat altogether, to leave the Heidlers.

Marya does not leave, and, although she has not yet slept with Heidler, the whole nature of their relationship has shifted. She has lunch with a young American writer by the name of Cairn, who expresses concern for her, but is too poverty-stricken himself to help her. He warns her of Heidler, but his inability to give anything but advice brings Marya even closer to a realisation that she is trapped both by the Heidlers themselves and her own lack of will.

Upon her return to the apartment, Heidler pleads his love once more, but Marya forestalls his advances by murmuring that she is afraid of being hurt again. Heidler tries to allay her fears and protests by telling her he wants to make her happy. Perhaps Heidler has touched an important element in spite of his self-interest when he tells Marya: 'You tear yourself to pieces over everything, and, of course, your fantastic existence has made you worse. You simply don't realise that most people take things calmly. Most people don't tear themselves to bits. They have a sense of proportion and so on.'(77)

The aimless nature of Marya's life has taken the balance and weight from most decisions and as a result panic and fear seize her at all points of conflict. Reasoned decision emanates from a sense of balance and values which give proportion to alternatives. These are qualities removed from Marya's life.

In this enclosed world of the Heidlers 'little Mado' is the eternal 'child', and the values which fashion, rule, and dominate this world remain opaque to her. As long as she lives in respectful obedience to the laws laid down she will be tolerated, but even here things are capricious and as long as she remains merely an object, she is passive before those human gods who establish the rules and the values by which the rules are laid down.

Lois insists Marya stay where she can watch over the affair, knowing full well that Marya must ride it out. A candid and revealing point in one of their conversations is Lois's remark, ' "D'you suppose that I care what you are, or think or feel? I'm talking about the man, the male, the important person, the only person who matters." '(81) It is to this female self-perspective that all of Rhys's heroines will fall victim—they reject it, but fall victim to its results. In a world where men are so valued, women are inescapably reduced to objects.

We realise that Lois—out of her humiliation and jealousy—has focused her anger on Marya rather than on Heidler, for Marya is a female, an adversary. For Lois, in spite of her 'advanced' ideas, masculine supremacy is a given, accepted as inevitable. It is this attitude on her part which forces Lois into the further self-humiliation of not only tolerating Heidler and Marya's affair, but condoning it in her presence and cajoling Marya into staying on with them. Lois believes she must help to gratify the male's need whatever the cost to her own person, for he is the superior being; the female must comply. Marya and Lois as females must be subservient to the dominant male, and the advantage of this subservience is measured by each in different ways: for Lois it brings recognition, position within the art world of Paris, it allows her to be confident and knowing; for Marya it offers a fundamental protection and security, or at least a temporary hospice from concern.

Although certainly no paragon of virtue herself, Marya is befuddled by the entire circumstances of the relationship with the Heidlers and Lois's acceptance of it. Like Heidler, Lois tells Marya she's '. . . making a fuss about nothing at all'.(82) After Lois leaves, Marya is possessed with 'a profound conviction of the unreality of everything'.(83) This dream-like reduction is consistent with Marya's passivity, for it allows her to move from compromising situation to situation without considering moral questions or fearing moral judgments. It is through this trance-like state that she accepts the present in isolation; she drifts into Heidler's arms and in the intensity of the moment immediately feels that 'all my life before I knew him was like being lost on a cold dark night'.(83) Marya is always ready to settle for the present, whatever its ultimate cost, if it obscures temporarily the unpleasant contours of life, but Lois sees the longer shadows and prepares for them. In a male dominated world, each has different needs: for Lois it is position and respect within the social order, for Marya it is immediate protection and fleeting enjoyment of the sensuous pleasures of life. In these different worlds each seeks her own false freedom.

In the early days of the love affair Marya is totally absorbed and happy, 'for perhaps the first time in her life. No past, No future. Nothing but the present: the flowers on the table, the taste of wine in her mouth.'(85) And in a curious way Lois is also happy with the situation. She recognises the people in the restaurant are aware of the *ménage à trois*, and 'instantly reacting to the atmosphere of sympathy and encouragement, sat very straight, dominating the situation and talking steadily in a cool voice'.(85)

Lois has adjusted to the relationship far better than Marya; Lois has reduced her to an object—a toy not only of Heidler, but her own toy too. Two remarks to Heidler illustrate how in her clever way she has perched on top of the triangle. First she suggests to Heidler that they must get Marya a new hat, 'she must do us credit'. Even more devastating for Marya, she suggests to Heidler: ' "Let's go to Luna-park after dinner," she said. "We'll put Mado on the joy wheel, and watch her being banged about a bit. Well, she ought to amuse us sometimes; she ought to sing for her supper; that's what she's here for, isn't it?" '(85)

One of the many lessons Rhys learned under the tutelage of Ford was the judicious selection of material, a stripping away of all but the essential. This lesson, of course, is of major importance to her style, but it also affects the arrangements of scenes and chapters. In *Quartet* we do not have the precision and synchronisation that is a part of the later works, but the clear direction of this important element of her art is established. For example, after the rather full depiction of Marya's early days in the Heidler household with its emerging tensions, there is not a further heaping of detail. Winter passes into spring and the next scene catches the full impact of the passage of time with a view of the affair from the eyes of an outsider, Cairn, the American writer who has again asked Marya to lunch. But Marya realises that Cairn has neither the wit nor experience to understand her situation, so she delivers an interior monologue which reveals in a most unadorned way her feelings: ' "Very well then, I will tell you. Listen. Heidler thinks he loves me and I love him. Terribly. I don't like him or trust him. I love him." '(92–93) She reveals her own feelings, and her estimation of the game they are all playing.

'D'you get me? And Lois says that she doesn't mind a bit and gives

us her blessing—the importance of sex being vastly exaggerated
and any little thing like that. But she says that I mustn't give her
away. So does Heidler. They call that playing the game. So I have
to trail around with them. And she takes it out of me all the time in
all sorts of ways. I can just keep my end up now, but soon I won't
be able to. And then, you see, I'm conscience-stricken about her.
I'm horribly sorry for her. But I know that she hasn't a spark of pity
for me. She's just out to down me—and she will.' (93)

We will see that interior monologues such as this become characteristic of Rhys's heroines. They reveal not only the feelings and
thoughts of the heroine, but also we recognise in them the inability of
these women to communicate their motivations and anxieties to
anyone. These monologues come to reveal an interior landscape, a
private world which is closed to human contact.

The whole arrangement with the Heidlers has become for Marya
an obsession of love and hatred. She is desolate and desperate, unable
to move the relationship in any way. Heidler brings her peace when
he makes love to her and comforts her, but these are only temporary
respites. As they ride to a summer place in the country, Marya looks
across the railway carriage and sees Lois, this 'formidable' figure, as
'obviously of the species wife'. (97) She glances from Lois to Heidler:
'and there he was, like the same chord repeated in a lower key'. (97–
8) They are inextricably together. Seeing this, Marya realises that she
is only a temporary fixture in their lives, a temporary cross for Lois
and passion for Heidler. Soon she would be discarded, no longer to be
'taken care of', 'and then they wanted to be excessively modern, and
then they'd think: "after all we're in Paris"'. (98) Marya is perceptive
in her assessment of the entire situation, and it is her understanding
that makes the whole thing impossible for her. She realises, too, that
she has no answer to their respective demands upon her: 'Of course,
there they were: inscrutable people, invulnerable people, and she
simply hadn't a chance against them, naïve sinner that she was.' (101)
'Naïve sinner'—it is from this self-characterisation that she justifies
her own seduction, her own willingness to play the game at all.
'Naïve' because the rules of the game emanate from protective
bourgeois values—rules too complex for her to grasp in the
beginning. The inevitable rupture of the *ménage à trois* occurs during a
visit to the country with charges and counter-charges.

Heidler in customary fashion reverts to his formulaic defense,
pleads drunkenness and retires, saying he'll remember nothing of this

tomorrow. The next morning Marya begins to pack and Lois attempts to help her and also apologises, but Marya has only hatred for her: 'She hated her air of guilt. She hated her eyes of a well-trained domestic animal.'(107) And it is precisely this aspect of Lois which Marya despises; yet Lois's submission offers the security and certitude that Marya knows she will never possess. In spite of her despicable cowering traits, they are the very ones which ultimately sustain Lois's place with Heidler and make her a necessary part of his life. As much as Marya, Lois is a victim of male subjugation; she has made herself able to fulfill a greater variety of male needs, but for all this she is no less violated by masculine domination. Both women are victims of that psychic and physical oppression which Simone de Beauvoir describes in *The Second Sex*, their consciousnesses are not defined in reciprocity with the male but as 'the other'. In containing only man's 'otherness', they are denied their own humanity. And the force of the novel moves increasingly, from this point on, to explore the abyss.

After this rupture Marya's life takes the tumble downward that fate and poor judgment had prescribed all along. With no other resources, she allows Heidler to set her up in a cheap hotel room, where he comes to visit her in 'an atmosphere of departed and ephemeral love [which] hung about the room like stale scent'.(111) She tells Heidler during one of his visits, after they make love: '"I feel as if I had fallen down a precipice."'(112) The narrative grows increasingly complex as it registers Marya's descent through a series of interrelated images and extended metaphors, developing a structural rhythm that provides a special perspective on Marya's movement and reactions as the events swarm around her. This added dimension is achieved through the style, and not only reflects with increasing intensity the full dimension of Marya's destruction, but also renders a deeper thematic resonance to the entire novel as it unfolds a larger vision through this complementary perspective.

Although the narrative focus still moves swiftly through the events, the realistic level is frequently blended with open ended images and dreamlike flights that are, nevertheless, rigidly controlled by the direct and simple style. The imagery and rhythm of this latter style renders the subtlety, dreamlike in quality, of Marya's consciousness which breaks from the realistic strains of the narrative and marks the psychological dimensions of her entrapment. These passages reveal far more of Marya's subconscious motives and anxieties than she herself can realise, and thus explore more profoundly the themes of the novel. On one level the narrative force seems to insist that

Marya's inability to break away from those upon whom she is dependent is justified, but on a deeper level the consciousness revealed to the reader points to a broader framework of human culpability and to the underlying reasons for Marya's desperation, her flight from reality into illusions, and her amoral posturing.

It is worthwhile to summarise briefly, at this point, the remaining narrative events of the novel which precipitate Marya's eventual fate. Throughout the summer Marya lies in her room, goes out to eat, and once a week visits Stephan in prison. Her routine is interrupted only by Heidler's visits to have sex. By August, however, Stephan is released, but he is allowed to remain in France for only a few days. He must go to Amsterdam to make connections, but he has no money to take her with him. Like a puppet on a string Marya is controlled by who has the money, and Heidler has the money. Torn between love and hate for Heidler, who has forbidden her to see Stephan, and loyalty to and despair over her relationship with Stephan, her choices become more and more restricted and her emotional state less and less stable. Heidler sends her to the south of France to 'recuperate' and provides her with only enough money to pay for her room and board. She sees her situation growing increasingly desperate, until a letter from Stephan brings 'a faint stirring of hope'.(165) After their reunion in Paris, Marya realises that Stephan's situation is such that he must strike out on his own. Marya reveals to Stephan that she had been Heidler's lover during his incarceration. Stephan's initial curiosity evolves into anger and thus begins a violent scene of cross-recriminations, finally ending with Stephan flinging Marya to the floor and walking out only to meet, fortuitously, an acquaintance and go off with her, either for just the night or perhaps to the Argentine.

The imagery in which Marya's sense of her dilemma is framed underscores her psychological vacillations and points, beyond her own awareness, to the inevitable consequences of her actions. The most persistent image is that of the caged animal. Its arrangement within the fabric of the narrative points out the significance of both the psychological and morally problematic elements of the novel and also, in a wider context, teases the ever-present post-Darwinian question of just how human beings stand in relation to animals: are we not after all similarly governed by laws over which we have no control, and are we not, with animals, brothers together locked in the same struggle for survival? The image with its predatory overtones and depiction of human confinement also imaginatively accommodates the various forms of conflict within *Quartet*.

The first time it appears is after Marya has moved in with the Heidlers, the day after H. J. has made clear to her that he intends for her to be his lover. With this prospect uppermost in her mind, she walks through Paris on a 'cloudless, intoxicating day'. She thinks of those days after Stephan's incarceration, remembering 'her tears and her submissions and the long hours she had spent walking between two rows of street lamps, solitary, possessed by pity as by a devil. "I've been wasting my life," she thought. "How have I stood it for so long?"'(74) Through self-pity she justifies the prospects of her submission to Heidler, excused by weakness and redeemed by helplessness. Although she has not allowed herself to become his lover, she justifies the prospect phychologically as a chance for new birth:

> And her longing for joy, for any joy, for any pleasure was a mad thing in her heart. It was sharp like pain and she clenched her teeth. It was like some splendid caged animal roused and fighting to get out. It was an unborn child jumping, leaping, kicking at her side.(74)

In this early stage the metaphor of the caged animal is not hostile because the entrapped has the resources of escape; it is a bold and natural act, uninhibited and free. However, a revealing aspect of the image is that of being acted upon rather than acting. Even joy comes by accepting.

The metaphor is seen in a different context when Marya visits Stephan in prison, and she exhorts him not to be so downtrodden about his circumstances. She says, ' "If anybody tried to catch me and lock me up I'd fight like a wild animal; I'd fight till they let me out or till I died."'(136) Stephan's reaction is unintentionally prophetic for Marya's own circumstance:

> 'Oh, no, you wouldn't, not for long, believe me. You'd do as the others do—you'd wait and be a wild animal when you came out.' He put his hand to his eyes and added: 'When you come out—but you don't come out. Nobody ever comes out.'
> She started at him, impressed by this phrase.(136)

'Impressed', because on the conscious level she is beginning to transfer his remarks to her own situation. And her 'stare' confirms her realisation. She quickly changes the subject, for it begins to dawn on her that one does not leave the cage merely by walking out of the unlocked gate. Instincts for survival and lust for life, so natural and pure in animals, are not sufficient protection for human beings with their conflicting motivations and complex feelings of guilt, joy, and despair. More importantly, we are reminded of the larger implications of this metaphor as it applies to the condition of the female generally, for Marya herself earlier referred to Lois as a 'well-trained domestic animal'.(107) This is the feminine condition in a sexist structure of male physical, social, economic, and psychological dominance. Marya's and Lois's imprisonment is no less real than Stephan's: and perhaps ugliest of all, this condition makes Lois what she is and provokes Marya to become what she has become. As de Beauvoir has written, 'It is not nature that defines women; it is she who defines herself by dealing with nature on her own account in her emotional life.'[2] But condemned to this oppression she is only an object, and since each consciousness must define itself as subject looking for reciprocity of relationship, achievement of freedom in the philosophical sense is impossible, whatever the physical comforts offered to the entrapped.

The metaphor for oppression is further extended as Marya's awareness of her dire circumstances increases. During her stay in Nice, she visits the zoo with the Heidler's friend, Miss Nicolson, and suggests they look at the animals:

> There was a young fox in a cage at the end of the zero—a cage perhaps three yards long. Up and down it ran, up and down, and Marya imagined that each time it turned it did so with a certain hopefulness, as if it thought that escape was possible. Then, of course, there were the bars. It would strike its nose, turn and run again. Up and down, up and down, ceaselessly. A horrible sight, really.(160)

She sees in the 'hopefulness' of the fox that same innocence and daring with which she entered into the affair with the Heidlers (it was with both, psychologically at least). It is through the bars that she sees with far more insight not only the hopelessness of her affair from the beginning, but partially, at least, the horror of its future implications. Although she will continue to raise false hopes and further justifications, at a deeper level she intuits the ramifications of her actions, this image confirming all the more conclusively the dire consequences of her relationship with the Heidlers.

This extended metaphor of entrapment acts as a barometer of Marya's deepest feelings and understanding of her situation with the Heidlers, but at each instance it carries a suggestiveness beyond her own understanding. At first, the image carries a hint of benevolence, for the cage is also protective, but as Marya's awareness increases, its malignant aspects become predominant. Marya, like the animal, is fed, clothed, and even catered to, but all of this is for the pleasure and whim of the one who holds the key, and, more particularly, the money—Heidler himself—the male. An important collateral for the cage metaphor throughout the latter half of the novel is the imagery accompanying the descriptions of hotel rooms which Marya occupies—paid for by Heidler. Although the narrative voice on the realistic level exposes Marya's feelings, the style itself, alternating from direct exposition to a metaphoral language, probes with equal subtlety the underlying conflicts of which Marya is only partially aware. The sentences in this latter mode remain short and direct, of simple construction, but a special effect is produced by a staccato force and by a sense of space between each construction.

Marya's desperation grows as events close in upon her. The metaphor of the caged animal, however, is not sufficiently complex to record her myriad emotions, nor are the wider observations of the narrative persona who records her condition in far bleaker terms:

> She was trying to climb out of the blackness up an interminable ladder. She was very small, as small as a fly, yet so heavy, so weighted down that it was impossible to hoist herself to the next rung. The weight on her was terrible, the vastness of space round her was terrible. She was going to fall. She was falling. The breath left her body.(162)

The cage has given way to a grotesque Kafkaesque image of claustrophobia and vertigo, reflecting Marya's horror, fear, dislocation, and desperation. This mutation of the image from animal to fly, with its greater intensity and emotional charge, reflects the closing in of the forces against her and her inability to cope with them.

The imagery records with growing forcefulness Marya's disembodiment and defeat; it also points to a condition which the realistic narrative only partially develops. These passages are more engrossing than a merely direct rendering of consciousness, for they are in a sense a stylisation of consciousness. The spatial element is further emphasised in the later stages of the novel by a dreamlike quality in the style which pervades the scrupulous surface realism.

Against her fears and the grim sense of foreboding, the narrator records Marya's construction of defense mechanisms based upon fantasies and delusions, through which the truism that extreme desire turns reality into fantasy echoes. Frequently these fantasies are brought on by more Pernod, 'After the fifth Pernod . . . "Never mind."'(160), or sleeping pills. The narrator tells us that drink brought upon Marya a temporary 'irrational feeling of security and happiness',(134) and as her condition becomes increasingly abject, she begins to build an elaborate refuge on her fantasies. Shunted off by Heidler, she creates an irrational image of Stephan as a savior:

Marya thought of her husband with a passion of tenderness and protection. He represented her vanished youth—her youth, her gaiety, her joy in life. She would tell herself: 'He was kind to me. He was awfully chic with me.'(125)

But these projections are desperate escape mechanisms and only serve to increase her despair, gradually giving way under a feeling of 'sickness' which leaves her lying in bed 'huddled with her arm over her eyes'.(125) Her fantasies run wild into obsessions which become increasingly intense:

She undressed, and all the time she was undressing it was as if Heidler were sitting there watching her with his cool eyes that confused and hurt her.

She lay down. For perhaps thirty seconds she was able to keep her mind a blank; then her obsession gripped her, arid, torturing, gigantic, possessing her as utterly as the longing for water possesses someone who is dying of thirst.(145)

Marya is unable to build any counter-universe against the grim and hostile world of her subjugation; once cut loose by Heidler and uncertain of her position with Stephan she is plunged into darkness. She is now in the world of absurd gestures and purposeless behaviour which Kafka describes. Stephan's rejection of her confirms with the most devastating directness her final violation and despair. All of her pathetic efforts to accommodate these opposing forces serve to confirm her own imprisonment and isolation in the masculine power structure.

One may argue that the intensity of the depiction of Marya's obsessional world has blurred the relationship between the narrator and the heroine, closed in on the aesthetic distance, and dismantled the objectivity necessary to render judgment on the world Marya inhabits. Seen in this light the novel is a work marred by self-indulgence and morbidity and offers no enlargement of vision and no real clarity of focus, only a chronicle of a weak victim's inevitable downfall. But to read the novel in this way is to misapprehend grossly the artistry embodied in *Quartet*. Its small canvas, through subtlety of style, probes the meaning of an enclosing world. There is not a single victim in this novel; all four of the major characters are victims; all are motivated by their lusts or needs and driven to a numbness and moral blindness in their hatreds, illusions, and self-pity. The two men are blind and uncaring and the women are little better, because in their desire for protection they become accomplices in a self-destructive and life-denying battle. The gross and subtle ways in which we hurt each other—it is around this subject that the themes of *Quartet* oscillate, not merely around Marya's pathetic downfall.

We become aware of this larger embodiment of theme as we experience the richness of the text and the formal relationship of its parts. For example, there is an adjustment of intimacy between the narrator-persona and the reader. As the relation of incident breaks off and the narrator records certain features of Marya's present condition, it is done not by altering stylistic structure, but through a shift in the quality of the tone, usually achieved through imagery of sharp and penetrating focus. Although these images are most frequently realised in the mind of the character, they take on a context beyond Marya as the style in which they are rendered fosters special intimacy between the narrator and reader. They are disciplined and controlled as they expand through the shaping stylistic arrangement. This technique, which becomes an increasingly dominant characteristic of Rhys's later work, is intricately related to the form of the entire novel, though it is apparent only to a limited extent in *Quartet*. Between the concentrated interiority of the text and the novel's brittle surface emerges a vision and a consistent tension which forms the basis for deep engagement between the reader and the work of art. It is through this unity that the themes of the novel expand, with the aesthetic realm more satisfying. The process for the reader becomes more a sense of shared discovery as the implications of the plot and narrative are embraced through a spatial, thematic, and formal ordering, thus affording an aesthetic whole and creating a far richer potential text for the reader.

The final scene brings together these various movements of the novel. It focuses on a violent quarrel between Stephan and Marya over her having slept with Heidler, and ends with Stephan's departure. Marya is left fallen and battered in what will become her permanent environment, a cheap hotel room—the habitat of the future of all Rhys's heroines, where they sleep, dream, drink, mechanically have intercourse, and are consumed by their helplessness in the world outside. Just before Stephan flings her to the floor, Marya has an epiphany emanating from her frustration and anger with Stephan:

> She began to laugh insultingly. Suddenly he had become the symbol of everything that all her life had baffled and tortured her. Her only idea was to find words that would hurt him—vile words to scream at him.(184)

Terrified by the bleak prospects of her future, and forced to confront them at last, she can no longer recede into a world of false dreams and hopes. Her obsessions are no longer dispelled by her fantasies. Stephan becomes the physical embodiment of all that they symbolise—he represents for her the masculine universe whose unwritten laws have controlled her. But even now she cannot fully apprehend this sudden revelation of feeling; her anger only searches for words of abuse. Marya remains 'baffled' by those who have 'tortured' her and left her pitilessly alone. The monsters who have claimed her, in the end, are without human faces; they are forces endemic to the structure of thought and social order to which Heidler and Stephan are also surely victims, for in the end all of the 'quartet' succumb to moral blindness and numbness.

If Marya is hypocritical, self-pitying and selfish, she is so because of the amoral world which she inhabits. Because she has been reduced to an object, it inevitably comes home to her with an awful force that her feelings really don't mean anything. There exists in Marya, to use Therese Benedek's term, a 'negative narcissism', where the female, treated exclusively as an object, reaches an emotional state in which the exclusive object of her psychic energy is the self and the emotions are depressive and painful. In a society which provides such easy victims, there can be no victors. Stephan is left to wallow in his self-pity, seeing women as 'loathsome' and 'horrible', 'soft and disgusting weights suspended round the necks of men, dragging them downwards. At the same time he longed to lay his head on Mademoiselle Chardin's shoulder and weep his life away.'(186) Out of this unhealthy mixture we find there is no capacity for reciprocal relationships with women, which further reminds us of the flimsy nature of Marya's initial hope. Stephan is the embodiment of male weakness and self-pity, but Heidler is a kind of incubus projection of the male species in his dominance and abuse of the female. With typical male hubris he laid out the rules of the game, and when Marya couldn't keep to them, she was merely released from her cage and left to stray as a wounded animal whose pleasure was no longer sought. Lois accepts the world of artificial rather than natural feelings; she bases her entire life on whatever the masculine code imposes upon her and as a result is a dehumanised accessory, who must play the servant's role at best, and at worst, the pimp. Her debasement is more complete; she is an active agent, an aggressor toward her own sex.

Quartet is a novel deeply suspicious of all human motivation; its themes centre upon deception, weakness, helplessness, and the cross-purposes of human beings as they seek their satisfactions or protection in a world that is at best apathetic but, more frequently, malignant. If the severely constricted world depicted in *Quartet* offers too limited a vehicle to explore the implications of these broader themes, the novel nevertheless achieves harmony through its penetrating vision of the central character and the world which she inhabits. Rhys's ample achievement in this novel can be too easily overlooked, and her characters and themes judged too morbid. The economy of language and directness of style can lead us to underestimate the range, depth, and quality of feeling in her work, where her narrative focus and technique relieve the intense subjectivity in *Quartet* and offer a dramatic, human portrait of the female consciousness in the modern world.

4 *After Leaving Mr Mackenzie* and *Voyage in the Dark*

Few serious British novels prior to those of Jean Rhys were so precisely sensitive to the unprotected woman—the female without the sinecures of money, family, or position. The best of these novels primarily concerned with women dealt with the attitudes, conditions, and forces which protected them, but left them isolated, frustrated, and unfulfilled. But the dominant themes of dependence, identity, and freedom emerged out of a milieu of security that was based upon conformity to a tacit but rigid structure of class and sex. Bloomsbury sensibility, for example, accommodated so well the limited world that society afforded the intelligent, sensitive female of the middle classes. Margaret Schlegel in E. M. Forster's *Howards End* is representative of a particular type of woman who struggled for harmony in a world dominated by values to which she was opposed. Her struggle to 'connect' pre-figures the later tests of Virginia Woolf's heroines. But, as Lionel Trilling pointed out, the struggle in *Howards End* 'is not between the classes but within a single class, the middle class. Neither the aristocracy nor the proletariat is represented and the very poor are significantly barred.'[1] The women in Rhys's novels live in a world far different from that depicted by Katherine Mansfield, Virginia Woolf, or even Dorothy Richardson; they are more vulnerable; there is less holding them together. The world which constricts and suffocates Rhys's heroines is harsher, more naked, far less sophisticated. Yet, while her perspective is different both in subject matter and, in some respects, theme, her heroines are ultimately enclosed in the same female world, and their imagination and consciousness formed by the experience of living in a society where their lives seem set apart, limited, and ultimately unresponsive to the rhythms of life.

In 1929 Virginia Woolf wrote an essay on 'Women and Fiction' in *The Forum* where she attempted to 'sum up the character of women's fiction at the present moment'. She went on to say that, 'it is courageous; it is sincere; it keeps closely to what women feel. It is not bitter'.[2] She does not mention by name any of the women writers she has in mind, but it is clear that the first two books of a young woman writer who had been living in Paris had not come to her attention. Woolf concludes her essay by looking to 'that fabulous age when women will have what has so long been denied them—leisure, and money, and a room to themselves'.[3] These are the same subjects that obsess Jean Rhys's heroines, for they have certainly not entered 'that fabulous age': they have a room to themselves, a series of rooms, but rather than giving them privacy and security, the rooms symbolise the drab, isolated, unprotected life of their occupants. In Woolf's fiction male oppression is more subtle than in Rhys's fiction, where male oppression is blatant at every level of activity, be it sexual, cultural, or economic.

The aestheticism of Bloomsbury, the experimentation and fictional worlds of writers such as May Sinclair or Dorothy Richardson, form interesting contrasts to the more destructive world depicted by Jean Rhys. Clarissa Dalloway sees her relationship to the universe as one of feeling, flow, with patterns emerging in moments of wholeness and harmony. Miriam Henderson in Richardson's *Pilgrimage* probes endlessly her interior life and the nature of feminine consciousness, and ultimately asserts its superiority over the masculine. Both of these female characters depict that inner life of feeling and sensibility which is set against the social and sexual determinants that historically prescribed such a narrow world. It is against this constricting world that Clarissa Dalloway, with social and monetary advantages, forms her consciousness. Her 'deeper feelings' seem to insure a place for her—to provide a 'room'. Miriam Henderson, on the other hand, is in touch with a broader spectrum of humanity than is Clarissa Dalloway, and she is more deeply concerned with her professional and intellectual role as a woman in society. Because of the constricted opportunities for a woman of talent, and the quality of mind traditionally associated with masculinity, Richardson's heroine begins to despise the masculine standards which exclude the female from full participation in the world, thus prescribing her very nature. Both Miriam Henderson and Clarissa Dalloway, although their social and economic positions are different, are products of the bourgeois world they inhabit; their values emanate from the same sources as their antagonism; their ultimate concern is to find their identities within an enlarged social and intellectual fabric free of sexual prejudice. In order to depict this struggle Woolf and Richardson, in spite of their many differences, broke with the traditional novel, as Sydney Kaplan observes of several modern British women novelists, 'by shifting their focus from the outer world to the inner, from the confident omniscient narrator to the limited point of view, from plot to patterning, and from action to thinking and dreaming . . . . They felt the need to consider consciousness not only as a means of organizing a novel but as a method for analyzing the minds of women and for attempting to define a specifically "feminine consciousness." '[4]

Although she shares many of the attitudes of a number of contemporary British women novelists, and her technical innovations achieved several of the same effects described by Kaplan, Rhys's heroines live in a world where the forms of life are distant from both Richardson's and Woolf's. They are without career ambitions, education, or the particular talents to compete in a world designed from masculine values and geared to masculine talents. Their movement within a closed and essentially deterministic universe is far more restricted. As we have recognised in Marya Zelli, the Rhys heroine is so suffocated and turned inward by the wretched life she lives, there is little spirit of rebellion, nor, as we see with Richardson's and Woolf's major female characters, is there an attempt at a philosophical formulation which compensates or redresses her condition. But this accommodation in the end does not liberate Woolf's or Richardson's characters, any more than it does Rhys's who are left without this apparent compensation. On the aesthetic level, as Elaine Showalter has so well observed:

> The fiction of Dorothy Richardson, Katherine Mansfield, and Virginia Woolf created a deliberate female aesthetic, which transformed the feminine code of self-sacrifice into an annihilation of the narrative self, and applied the cultural analysis of the feminists to words, sentences, and structures of language in the novel. Their version of modernism was a determined response to the material culture of male Edwardian novelists like Arnold Bennett and H. G. Wells, but, like D. H. Lawrence, the female aestheticists saw the world as mystically and totally polarized by sex. For them, female sensibility took on a sacred quality, and its exercise became a holy, exhausting, and ultimately self-destructive rite, since woman's receptivity led inevitably to suicidal vulnerability.

Paradoxically, the more female this literature became in the

formal and theoretical sense, the farther it moved from exploring
the physical experience of women. Sexuality hovers on the fringes
of the aestheticists' novels and stories, disguised, veiled and denied.
Androgyny, the sexual ethic of Bloomsbury and an important
concept of the period, provided an escape from the confrontation
with the body. Erotically charged and drenched with sexual
symbolism, female aestheticism is nonetheless oddly sexless in its
content. Again, 'a room of one's own,' with its insistence on artistic
autonomy and its implied disengagement from social and sexual
involvement, was a favorite image.[5]

In contrast to these novels which deliberately built a female aesthetic
and carefully avoided the physical aspects of female sexuality and
awareness, Rhys's fiction is deeply absorbed with this basic aspect of
life. Although her heroines are passive and the sexual act itself is
hardly erotic, Rhys deals constantly with the nature of the
psychological relationship between men and women. Treatment of
this dimension of the male—female relationship reveals nearly as
much about her male characters as it does the females. This open
treatment of sexuality in Rhys's fiction deepens her treatment of the
consciousness of her heroines, a comprehensiveness shared neither by
Woolf's nor Richardson's heroines.

The two novels which followed *Quartet, After Leaving Mr
Mackenzie* (1931) and *Voyage in the Dark* (1934),[6] amplify and enrich
Rhys's vision of the feminine consciousness. Furthermore, each
reveals the increasing technical competence and richness of her style.
Her rendering of plot and theme becomes more unified as her novels
penetrate those aspects of a woman's nature which had eluded the
modern British novel. Because the world of her heroines is in the end
so confined, and because her canvas is relatively small, it is difficult to
make large claims for her breadth of vision, but as these two novels
reveal, Rhys's portraits, because of the imaginative energy lying
behind them and the distinctive style which exposes them, are
masterpieces of a kind. Perhaps because their focus and dimension are
so well controlled and limited, they achieve a unity and aesthetic
power beyond the narrow experience of their heroines, enabling us to
discern the shadow-play of social and moral issues. Even though her
heroines are little people without large ideas or much purpose, and
often feckless, they are real, forged by an understanding of the world
and an artistic vision in sympathy with their condition.

At this stage of her career the imagination in Rhys's work divorces itself from what actually happened in her own life, and she is able to use first person narration without endangering aesthetic distance through too narrow a vision or special pleading. The experiences of Anna Morgan, the young heroine of *Voyage in the Dark*, are taken from Jean Rhys's own early days in England, after she had left the RADA and had begun to tour the provincial towns with a theatrical company. The events are largely drawn from notebooks and diaries which she kept during this formative period. The narrative strategies and the dual focus which she was to develop were not fully conceived, however, until she returned to this material after the completion of *Mr Mackenzie*. Because the autobiographical elements precede both *Quartet* and *Mr Mackenzie*, the novel is especially important in further delineating the portrait of the Rhys heroine; besides its own intrinsic merit, *Voyage* gives more shape to the heroines of the two novels which preceded it and its Caribbean background anticipates the fully developed exoticism of *Wide Sargasso Sea*. Since the autobiographical material she was to use for *Voyage* was sufficiently distant to give emotional and artistic focus to the story, Rhys wisely chose the intimacy of a first person narrator. The nature of the narrative, which called for recollection and recreation of childhood experience on the part of the main character, made an 'I' narrator especially appropriate. This first person narration accommodates the most important structural feature of the novel, Anna Morgan's memories of her childhood in the West Indies. Young Anna reveals herself to us in a way very different from Marya Zelli and Julia Martin of *Mr Mackenzie*, for while Anna is experiencing the present events of the plot, she is also the figure who ultimately narrates those events. We have in *Voyage*, because of Rhys's structuring technique, a triple level of observation: first, the experiencing self, Anna's life in the narrative present; second, the narrative self that is distant from the events; and, third, the self of Anna's memory who is recalled in dream or conscious recollection and who experiences the events of child-hood in the Carribbean. The function of this last narrative process is not only crucial to the novel's theme, but is of fundamental importance to the characterisation and meaning. Although erected from the single perspective of the 'I' narrator, these reflections into Anna's past also provide a sense of movement and evoke the novel's central image of a voyage, both inward and outward. They also form a spatial construction of Anna's world.

Without this element of memory and the dynamic resonance it creates, the novel would simply stand as a well-told but pathetic little tale of a young girl who comes to England from the West Indies and gets a job as a chorus girl with a provincial touring company, falls in love with a wealthy young man in London and becomes his mistress. She is eventually disposed of by him and, through naïveté and lack of initiative, falls into compromising circumstances, attracts a succession of lovers, becomes pregnant, and gets money from her first lover to have her abortion. A series of beautifully constructed memory frames, however, blend into the narrative and set up a cumulative and complex process of awareness, giving depth, richness, and moral focus to the novel. Anna's memories are exclusively of her life on the Island and they are characterised by a sharpness of detail which forms a careful contrast to the dreamy quality of her present life in England as she relates it.

In the opening lines of the novel Anna depicts the basic difference between the two worlds:

> It was as if a curtain had fallen, hiding everything I had ever known. It was almost like being born again. The colours were different, the smells different, the feeling things gave you right down inside yourself was different. Not just the difference between heat, cold; light, darkness; purple, grey. But a difference in the way I was frightened and the way I was happy. I didn't like England at first. I couldn't get used to the cold. Sometimes I would shut my eyes and pretend that the heat of the fire, or the bed-clothes drawn up round me, was sun-heat; or I would pretend I was standing outside the house at home, looking down Market Street to the Bay. When there was a breeze the sea was millions of spangles; and on still days it was purple as Tyre and Sidon. Market Street smelt of the wind, but the narrow street smelt of niggers and woodsmoke and salt fishcakes fried in lard. (When the black women sell fishcakes on the savannah they carry them in trays on their heads. They call out, 'Salt fishcakes, all sweet an' charmin', all sweet an' charmin'.') It was funny, but that was what I thought about more than anything else—the smell of the streets and the smells of frangipanni and lime juice and cinnamon and cloves, and sweets made of ginger and syrup, and incense after funerals or Corpus Christi processions, and the patients standing outside the surgery next door, and the smell of the sea breeze and the different smell of the land-breeze. (7-8)

From the beginning she tells us that the contrast for her is far deeper than the matter of simple and obvious opposites. The entire psychology, the deeper structures of civilisation, are fundamentally opposed. The strong olfactory images which dominate these initial memories underscore the primal nature of Anna's Island experience and her deep attachment to it that endures in the cold and darkness of England.

Throughout the novel there is never a scene in England depicted with such clarity and vividness. In this opening paragraph and in many of the memory images of her home in the Caribbean which follow, the language reaches out to assimilate what it seeks to describe. For Anna this world clearly has a balance and meaning reflected in the style in which it is recalled. Her description of her life in England, on the other hand, is frequently vague and dislocated: 'I felt as if I had gone out of myself, as if I were in a dream.'(23)

The interior movement in Anna's mind between England and the West Indies is so frequent and her memories of the latter so vivid that present and past often seem to operate on the same level. From the beginning Anna warns us that she frequently confuses the reality of the two: 'Sometimes it was as if I were back there and as if England were a dream. At other times England was the real thing and out there was the dream, but I could never fit them together.'(8)

It is from this inability of Anna to fit the experiences of both worlds together into her life that the novel surely derives its title. Her life in the Islands, for all its richness, failed to prepare her for the harder, colder England. Her voyage is one of darkness, and one which seems to carry her further and further away from those vital qualities of life that seemed to exist in the Islands. She does not, however, reflect upon her experiences with the debilitating emotion of nostalgia, for life as she recalls it there was not without conflict and peril; but it seemed to be lived in harmony with nature and natural forces—a rhythm of life was established where one felt attuned to one's natural impulses rather than crippled by and subservient to a motion of life that seemed alien and hostile, and ultimately life-denying.

The development of these memory images gradually reveals a pattern and an accretive meaning. Moreover, the narrative's dual focus on present and past invigorates the entire book as the two opposed worlds meet in Anna's experience, and the narrational self attempts to draw meaning from the personal struggle of the confrontation. It is in this matrix of both worlds that the deeper meaning of Anna's failure lies.

As these memories blend with Anna's contemporary situation they

add greater dimension to her stature as a character and further define
her nature. After she has met the man who is to become her first lover,
Walter Jeffries, she is taken ill. She and Walter have not yet been
together physically when she writes to him with an appeal to visit her.
As she awaits his reply, she lies in bed and recalls Francine, the black
woman who took care of her during a childhoold illness. She
remembers, too:

> I wanted to be black, I always wanted to be black. I was happy
> because Francine was there, and I watched her hand waving the fan
> backwards and forwards and the beads of sweat that rolled from
> underneath her handkerchief. Being black is warm and gay, being
> white is cold and sad.(31)

There are two important aspects to this early memory: first, Anna's
recollection of her continuing desire to be black, to become one with
a culture—to possess a racial heritage which seemed in natural
harmony with life; second, the image of Francine as a comforter and
protector. This memory image is interrupted by the appearance of
Walter standing in the doorway. He quickly calls a doctor and rushes
out for 'an eiderdown and a bottle of burgundy and some grapes and
Brand's essence of beef and a cold chicken'.(33) Walter becomes her
protector and comforter, a kind of surrogate father. When she
recovers and goes to bed with Walter for the first time, she associated
with him a kind of primal, non-carnal, human warmth: 'When I got
into bed there was warmth coming from him and I got close to him.
*Of course you've always known, always remembered, and then you forget so
utterly, except that you've always known it. Always—how long is
always?'*(37, italics in text) Admittedly, this passage, because of its
nonreferential language, is open to a number of interpretations, but
the context associates Walter with the warmth and protection of
Anna's childhood in the West Indies.

A number of other equally important elements are also present in
these memory interludes. There is, for example, a frequent inter-
mingling of Roman Catholic religious ritual which seems in a
curious way to Anna to blend in with the vividness of the Caribbean
atmosphere. She recalls preparing for Mass on Sunday, and kneeling
in the church biting 'the back of the pitchpine pew in front'.(42) Anna
later tells Walter more of her life on the Island and mentions seeing a
slave-list at her mother's family estate, and she remembers a name
from the list, 'Maillotte Boyd, aged 18, mulatto, house servant',(53)

and later makes sense of the memory by association with a remembered Church service. One night after she and Walter have made love, Anna lies in bed remembering a sermon on the Four Last Things and again recalls the name of the slave, Maillotte Boyd. She identifies with the slave girl on a number of levels, her early death as she imagines her own, her mixed blood which resembles her own profound communal separation that has left her culturally and emotionally excluded from both racial heritages—torn away from one and unable to adapt to the other. As she lies in Walter's bed, she further associates Maillotte's slavery with her own.

As the novel traces Anna's unhappiness and dislocation a number of female figures play prominent roles in bringing about her pathetic demise. Her contemporaries exploit her and use her, but there is a more significant female who looms malignantly. This is the character of Aunt Hester, who brought her to England after her father's death. Hester is important in the overall scheme of the narrative: she is Anna's last human link with her life in the Islands, and her tacit rejection of Anna symbolises her final severence from familial ties as well as her plunge into an unprotected environment. It was Hester who tore her away from a culture she knew and understood and now leaves her to drift unprepared and alone. Hester is a self-righteous moral villain whose treatment of Anna foreshadows the advantage taken of her by other women later in the novel.

At the novel's centre, however, is Anna's devastating affair with Walter Jeffries. Anna's simple naïveté draws her to him and he plays the role of seducer with consummate skill. Anna notices that, 'he didn't look at my breasts or my legs, as they usually do. Not that I saw. He looked straight at me and listened to everything I said with a polite and attentive expression, and then he looked away and smiled as if he had sized me up.'(13–14) Upon leaving, Walter invites Anna to dinner when she next returns to London, and with this prospect there is already a small change in Anna: 'We went out into the street to say good-bye to them. I was thinking it was funny I could giggle like that because in my heart I was always sad, with the same sort of hurt that the cold gave me in my chest.'(15) A similar giddy feeling returns to Anna when she and Walter meet in London. He makes a pass at her and she fends him off angrily; he apologises, allows her to rest, and then sends her home in a taxi. The awkwardness of this first meeting is well controlled by the pointed dialogue, and the scene ends in a silly triumph for Anna, her virtue left intact and Walter still pursuing. Anna thinks as they go out into the streets to flag the taxi,

'"The girls would shriek with laughter if I were to tell them this. Simply shriek."'(24) But it does not take Walter long to violate her. On her next visit he takes her to bed and afterwards confirms his view of the relationship by putting money in her purse:

> My handbag was on the table. He took it up and put some money into it. Before he did it he looked toward me but he thought I couldn't see him. I got up. I meant to say, 'What are you doing?' But when I went up to him, instead of saying, 'Don't do that,' I said, 'All right, if you like—anything you like, anyway you like.' And I kissed his hand.
> 'Don't,' he said. 'It's I who ought to kiss your hand, not you mine.'(38)

It dawns on Anna what she is to him, as she leaves the taxi, 'When I paid the man he winked at me. I looked over his head and pretended not to notice.' (39) Anna's violation is complete, and the remainder of the novel traces her downward path. And as we follow her I am reminded of that phrase somewhere in Graham Greene's *The Quiet American*, 'innocence always calls mutely for protection'.

The narrative force of the book renders Anna's situation inevitable, without real options. As we have seen with Marya Zelli, this condition without recourse becomes the typical plight of the Rhys heroine. The options seem to be so narrow, the alternatives so similar, the woman's role so fixed that her only choice is to choose under whose disposition she should fall. It is precisely out of this condition and those similar to it that the consciousness of the character seems to be formed.

Not Walter, but Walter's cousin, Vincent, writes the inevitable patronising, self-protective epistle, informing Anna of Walter's decreasing affection for her. The tone from the beginning is appalling:

> My dear Anna,
>   This is a very difficult letter to write because I am afraid I am going to upset you and I hate upsetting people. We've been back for nearly a week but Walter hasn't been at all well and I have persuaded him to let me write to you and explain matters. I'm quite sure you are a nice girl and that you will be understanding about this. Walter is still very fond of you but he doesn't love you like that any more . . .(92–3)

There is the promise of money if she handles it well and, of course, returns the letters Walter has sent to her. The affair ends on the same basis that it began; Anna has merely been used and is now being disposed of when the male grows tired or fearful. The betrayal is complete.

The depth of Anna's reaction to the letter from Vincent is conveyed through an image she recalls from her childhood. Upon receiving the letter she remembers coming upon her Uncle Bo when she was a young girl. He is sleeping on the verandah with his mouth open. As she approaches him she sees that 'long yellow tusks like fangs come out of his mouth and protruded down to his chin'.(92) She relates, 'I had never seen false teeth before not to notice them.'(92) Vincent's letter conjures up this image again. She thinks, 'But what's the matter with me? That was years and years ago, ages and ages ago. Twelve years ago or something like that. What's this letter got to do with false teeth?'(92)

After she rereads the letter, she thinks, '"What the hell's the matter with me? I must be crazy. This letter has nothing to do with false teeth."'(94) It, of course, has everything to do with false teeth, especially when we recall Uncle Bo's own letter that Hester has read to her, and that startling mask-like image of the sleeping male figure with yellow fangs. Present and past experience interpret each other for Anna. Drawing as it does from her childhood memory, the image symbolises a whole complex of emotions and feeling. It links her betrayal by Walter to Uncle Bo's rejection of her. The sleeping picture of Bo is like a horrible mask, and the letter is also an inadvertently ugly mask. The mask and the letter work in reverse; they reveal rather than hide ugliness. The power of the image suggests to Anna that appearances are never to be trusted, for they mask human cruelty and abuse only for as long as it is convenient. Anna is so devastated by the letter that she is unable to recognise the fullness of the image's range of meaning, nor is her psyche able to come to terms with its implications. Gradually, however, it becomes for her an awful knowledge and eventually shapes her view of the world.

As we have seen, this fluctuation throughout the novel between Anna's childhood in the West Indies and her life in London is far more than a simple device to generate rhythm and set up contrasts. These earlier reflections by the 'I' narrator create a fictional mode whereby the experiencing self of the novel is revealed beyond its contemporary context. Together present and past create a kind of dual passage or voyage which has, for Anna, merged into a dreamlike world that has

left her unable to define experience. Her development through West
Indian childhood is constantly set against the London present to create
not only a tension and strong narrative reasonance within the novel,
but also to expand its social and human dimensions. The two
experiences as they merge give coherence to the fictive world of the
novel, both epistemological and moral. Although Anna is unable to
reconcile her past with the present, remaining a fish out of water, this
fictional strategy provides the thematic resolution or the novel as we
see Anna's oscillation between the world of reflected experience and
present circumstances.

We as readers must take the necessary adjustments to accommodate these shifts of setting, time, and culture, for they provide the
transcendent meaning of Anna's experience and render thematic
coherence to the novel. Structured in this way *Voyage in the Dark*
pursues a dialectic between Anna's present and past, home and exile,
blacks and whites, childhood and maturity. The warm, lazy, exotic,
natural world of the West Indies, which is surely the essence of her
nature, failed to prepare her for the Anglo-Saxon world into which
she was cast adrift. These memory images of childhood are not
benign, but they reveal an organic connection of the self with nature
that gave her an identity—an identity which is now fractured in the
urban world of London. Anna's experience is clearly the story of
exile, a theme recurring again and again in twentieth-century
literature, and as much as any other illuminates an essential aspect of
the modern experience. Different from the predominant male angst
of the age, the female's struggle, as Rhys portrays it, is more basic
because she has less and frequently contends with cruder torment—
denied the luxury of a philosophical outcry because she is too engaged
in the struggle for physical and psychological existence.

In an important passage near the end of the novel, Anna remembers
the long road she took as a little girl to her mother's old homestead,
the Constance Estate. The journey begins amid the lush forest with
the sea below: 'You ride in a sort of dream, the saddle creaks
sometimes, and you smell the sea and the good smell of the
horse.'(151) The passage concludes:

> It took three hours to get to Constance Estate. It was as long as a life
> sometimes. I was nearly twelve before I rode it by myself. There
> were bits in the road that I was afraid of. The turning where you
> came very suddenly out of the sun into the shadow; and the shadow
> was always the same shape. And the place where the woman with

yaws spoke to me. I suppose she was begging but I couldn't understand because her nose and mouth were eaten away; it seemed as though she were laughing at me. I was frightened; I kept on looking backwards to see if she was following me, but when the horse came to the next ford and I saw clear water I thought I had forgotten about her. And now—there she is.(151−2)

This journey captures symbolically Anna's entire life, for amid all the expectation and natural beauty the harsher reality of this diseased being shadows her at the end, no matter how many short intervals between its disappearences. The passage's full meaning clarifies Anna's fate at the end of the novel as she lies in bed after her abortion:

When their voices stopped the ray of light came in again under the door like the last thrust of remembering before everything is blotted out. I lay and watched it and thought about starting all over again. And about being new and fresh. And about mornings, and misty days, when anything might happen. And about starting all over again, all over again . . . . (187−8)

'Starting all over again' becomes the central concern of Rhys's older heroines as they suffer similar defeats. This hope, however elusive, seems to be all that keeps them going, and eventually even this will be replaced with a resigned clarity of vision which depends less upon hope than the more natural, if less enobling, instinct of survival. And all of this is a process of awareness of the world and the formation of consciousness.

This growing awareness on Anna's part by the end of the novel, however, raises an important crux in the composition of the nature of the Rhys heroine. Particularly, why did Anna not go back to the theatre, take the lessons and make the contracts that Walter would have provided her? As her later heroines will relate, somehow their will has been crushed; they can no longer compete in the world on their own. Rather, they will give themselves up to the more desperate but immediately easier struggle for survival by finding the protection of another male, and another. The road they choose is a rough and dehumanising one, for they have found the source of male vanity in its most naked and repellent aspects.

Comparable images, comparable mannerisms of the heroines, comparable drifts into a nether world of somnambulistic escape, unite *Voyage in the Dark* and *After Leaving Mr Mackenzie*. Their particular genesis allows us to read them reflexively; they expand and deepen each other. Although *Mr Mackenzie* was published before *Voyage*, its heroine, Julia Martin, is older, harder, more ravaged by the world than Anna. Julia has seen and experienced more, is a creature of greater complexity than her younger counterpart. She is more resiliant and combative. Also, Rhys's prose has focused on its subject matter: nuance, understatement, precise depiction of the vicissitudes of mind and emotion of a woman unable to cope with her fate but at the same time remarkably committed to survival in spite of all the odds, even those which her very nature poses against her.

The world is older in *Mr Mackenzie*, and its annihilating forces more visible, more easily discerned, more undeniable. Incident yields significance more clearly, but also more subtly because the participants are more experienced and knowing. Their cynicism marks their impotence, but it reveals their knowledge of themselves and each other and it also brings to the surface their baser motives. The characters in *Mr Mackenzie* have been to the human well and have seen dust instead of their reflections. The idea of mutual sharing between a man and a woman has long since evaporated. All of the initial disillusionments are over. At the end of *Voyage* Anna lies in bed thinking about starting over again, but at the end of *Mr Mackenzie* Julia knows that for her it is 'the hour between dog and wolf',(191) that time of neither daylight nor darkness, where end and beginning are indistinguishable, the earth's rotation the only certainty.

Mr Mackenzie is a precisely formed and structured novel, compressed and relentless in its intimate portrayal of a woman fighting off the nadir of her existence, her barren life somehow staying afloat in desperation. We encounter in this novel in more precisely human terms the cross-purposes of men's and women's behaviour toward each other—the self-protection that each seeks as he or she parries for advantages over the other. *Mr Mackenzie* expands the psychological surface of Rhys's fiction, because it treats masculine motivation and explores the interiority of male deception and need for sexual conquest. Our concerns in the study of this novel are threefold: to look more closely at the interior world of the heroine, study the behaviour of the two male characters, and look once again into the relationship between woman, a relationship that is constant, although circumstances change its manifestations.

The novel is composed of three clearly delineated parts, setting and environment forming more than the superficial divisions; the cities of Paris and London are important geographical and psychological poles

for the Rhys heroine. Part I is set in Paris after Julia has been disposed
of by Mr Mackenzie. The second and longest section is set in London
where Julia visits her sister and tries to attend to her dying mother,
develops her abortive relationship with Mr Horsfield whom she has
met in Paris, and visits and receives money from an old lover who
makes it clear that this is the last time she can come to him. The brief
final section of the novel covers Julia's return to Paris. The novel
traces Julia's constant search for money, but, on a deeper level, is
concerned with her quest for some human engagement. She is a
woman so long isolated and yet so dependent that nearly every
human contact seems doomed before it has begun. *Mr Mackenzie* is a
novel, too, of ghosts, ghosts out of Julia's own past which torment
her, broken relationships with her family and ill-fated affairs. She is
herself a ghost. When she writes her old lover in London, she closes by
saying, 'I hope you won't think of me as an importunate ghost.'(66)
Her first day in London she walks through the fog in Tottenham
Court Road:

> The houses and the people passing were withdrawn, nebulous.
> There was only a grey fog shot with yellow lights, and its cold
> breath on her face, and the ghost of herself coming out of the fog to
> meet her.
>   The ghost was thin and eager. It wore a long, very tight check
> skirt, a short dark-blue coat, and a bunch of violets bought from
> the old man in Woburn Square. It drifted up to her and passed her
> in the fog. And she had the feeling that, like the old man, it looked at
> her coldly, without recognizing her.(67–8)

This ghost of herself haunts her throughout the novel. Ghostlike
figures emerge frequently during her ten-day stay in London; they
grimly point to not only her past but, forebodingly, to her present
and future. These totem figures of death constantly appear as she
walks the streets. In a restaurant the man next to her proclaims: '"A
most extraordinary thing! I've just seen a man I thought was dead."'
Julia asks, '"Were you pleased to see him?"'(69) Her own return to
London is a return from the dead. We gradually realise that Julia's
journey is both forward and backward, but further discovery seems
to lie in neither direction. Although it seems incredibly obvious by
now, Rhys's subject is failure, and in *Mr Mackenzie* this fundamental
theme is fully developed.
   The novel's opening scene, with its precisely constructed picture of

Julia's constricted physical and psychological world, exemplifies the nature of her defeat. As we contemplate the description of this enclosed, inner world which Julia has created after Mr Mackenzie's departure, we are reminded of Simone de Beauvoir's remark that 'there are few crimes that entail worse punishment than the generous fault of putting one's self entirely in another's hands'.[7] And this is precisely what Julia has done.

The Paris hotel where Julia is staying, the landlady with the smelly cats, the room, its prospects, all of its features and contents are described with great accumulation of detail holding significance for us as they do for Julia. They have a private meaning for her. We begin to realise that we are in the middle of a self-imposed universe, and her response to all of its interior features, whether they be pictures, beds, or wallpaper, are indicative of Julia's anxieties and state of mind. The objects are privately, reflectively symbolic. She hated, for example, the still life oil painting on the wall:

> It shared, with the colour of the plush sofa, a certain depressing quality. The picture and the sofa were linked in her mind. The picture was the more alarming in its perversion and the sofa the more dismal. The picture stood for the idea, the spirit, and the sofa stood for the act.(11)

To all the aspects of this microcosm of the universe, she has assigned values and, in doing so, she has attempted to create a world with no human intrusions—a world exclusively of the self. From the beginning we are aware, just as Julia is, that all of this is a flimsily constructed cage, but, nevertheless, 'it was a good sort of place to hide in'.(11) She had taken the room six months earlier and told herself that she would stay there until the 'sore' and 'cringing' feeling, which was the legacy of Mr Mackenzie, departed. She is aware from the beginning therefore that she has only a temporary hospice from the world outside, only so long as Mackenzie's three-hundred franc cheques arrive each week. She remains, even after he has disposed of her, at his mercy and dependent upon his largesse. As Sasha Jansen, the heroine of *Good Morning, Midnight* will proclaim, 'a room is a place where you hide from the wolves outside and that's all any room is'.[8] Its limited value Julia realises, too, and this makes her attempt all the more desperate.

In this enclosed refuge, however, Julia is seemingly able to lick her wounds, sink quietly into the temporary obivion of the ever-present bottle, and deceive herself into feeling she is keeping the wolves away. In her private world she even finds some comfort in 'memories'. But these are memories which reflect the artificial enclosure she has created: they are those of an 'old woman' who awaits death. This desperately individualised creation has left her mind 'a confusion of memory and imagination'.(12) She grows increasingly disoriented and imagines herself being enveloped by the outside world: 'The rumble of life outside was like the sound of the sea which was rising gradually around her.'(12) The defensive narcissism which we see in Julia in these opening pages, together with the image of drowning, confirms the utter helplessness of her plight. We are aware from the beginning that she is attempting to create a private fantasy world where she can order and manage her experience, but in the inevitable scheme of things this is impossible. And perhaps more than anything else, we learn in this opening scene of Julia's lack of affinity for any other human being: 'She hardly ever thought of men, or of love.'(12)

Julia is bereft of those characteristics which give people an identity:

> Her career of ups and downs had rubbed most of the hall-marks off her, so that it was not easy to guess at her age, her nationality, or the social background to which she properly belonged.(14)

The narrator also tells us she is unable to live by her wits: 'By her eyes and the deep circles under them you saw that she was a dreamer, that she was vulnerable—too vulnerable ever to make a success of a career of chance.'(14) Although it may reveal itself in a superficial vanity, there is, however, a quality of self-respect and endurance in Julia:

> She made herself up elaborately and carefully, yet it was clear that what she was doing had long ceased to be a labour of love and had become partly a mechanical process, partly a substitute for the mask she would have liked to wear.
>
> To stop making up would have been a confession of age and weariness. It would have meant that Mr Mackenzie had finished her. It would have been the first step on the road that ended in looking like that woman on the floor above—a woman always dressed in black, who had a white face and black nails and dyed hair which she no longer dyed, and which had grown out for two inches into a hideous pepper-and-salt grey.(14)

This is the first description of what we begin to see as inherent resiliency; it is also the source of a carelessness and restlessness which curiously enough becomes an important defence in the inevitable sexual power-relationships that men impose upon her. Her resiliency is a source of self-respect but far from bringing any salvation, it is a further source of her anguish: for it is proof, Julia's only consistent source of self-respect-resiliency requires conditions leading to self-destruction.

The expansion of our understanding of the Rhys heroine does not occur exclusively, however, in the novel's treatment of this interior world of Julia Martin, but rather in the amplitude Rhys gives to the exploration of Julia's relationship with the other male and female characters in novel. For a number of reasons Rhys was able in *Mr Mackenzie* to explore far more thoroughly the dimensions of the male—female relationship, technically through a subtle shifting of point of view, and thematically by moving inside the mental and psychological process of the male characters. This, of course, also adds a dramatic quality to the book that heretofore she achieved through quickly shifting scenes, rapid movement of plot, and an episodic structure. Rhys's willingness to construct her novel in such a way as to allow her narrative entry into the male consciousness also gives further dimension to her heroine; other characters interpret her, and this achieves in *Mr Mackenzie* more narrative distance between the author-persona and the heroine than had been achieved in her previous novels. She achieves in this novel a distance from her heroine, and as we know aesthetic distance affects the entire mode of narration.

We were privy to Heidler's posturing and elaborate self-justifications in *Quartet*, but through the observations of an outsider, superficial when compared with the insights into the male psyche in *Mr Mackenzie*. Mr Mackenzie is on stage far less than Heidler, but his characterisation is richer and the narration more penetrating in this novel. After Mackenzie's attorney sends Julia a letter enclosing 1,500 francs, the last payment on the debt of a broken love affair, Julia sets out to confront him. The prospect of this assumes for Julia the dimensions of a confrontation with the whole social order:

At the sight of him Julia's heart began to beat furiously and her legs trembled. She was excited to an almost unbearable degree, for, added to her other emotions, was the fact that she was very much afraid both of him and of his lawyer. When she thought of the combination of Mr Mackenzie and Maître Legros, all sense of reality deserted her and it seemed to her that there were no limits at all to their joint powers of defeating and hurting her. Together, the two perfectly represented organized society, in which she had no place and against which she had not a dog's chance.(22)

Filled with humiliation and rage, Julia spies Mackenzie seated in the restaurant, but the narration immediately shifts focus and the whole scene with the two of them is rendered from his point of view. This device serves several purposes: it enables us to see Julia from another angle, but, more importantly, it reveals male motivation and enlarges upon the external social source of Julia's angst. Mackenzie, too, has created a defensive world; 'he had adopted a certain mental attitude, a certain code of morals and manners. . . .'(24) The great difference between Julia's privately constructed world and Mackenzie's is that 'his code was perfectly adapted to the social system'.(24) Mackenzie's 'code, philosophy or habit of mind' which insulates him from emotions and impulses 'would have been a complete protection to him had it not been for some kink in his nature . . . which morbidly attracted him to strangeness, to recklessness, even unhappiness'.(24) But even when this 'kink' impelled him to drop his barriers, 'his business instinct came to his help, and he got out undamaged'.(24) With the same moral blindness as Tom Buchanan in *The Great Gatsby*, Mackenzie can retreat into his money from the indelicate task of picking up the pieces.

Mackenzie sees this 'kink' in his nature which expressed itself in a sexual attraction for Julia as, 'part of the insanity for which he was not responsible'.(25) Ironically enough, these moments of lust or wild passion, however base, afford him his only real human contact. He is only drawn out of his enclosed, ordered world by sexual obsession: 'Why did I want to sleep with her? Yet there was no getting away from it; for a time she had obsessed him. He had lied; he had made her promises which he had never intended to keep; and so on, and so on.'(25) As his immediate lust waned he began to pull away and retreat into his well insulated world which protects him from the unwanted intimacy of a close relationship with a woman. The following passage describes how Julia's revelations and intimacy awaken in him the ultimately stronger instincts of self-preservation:

On another occasion she had said, 'You see, a time comes in your life when, if you have any money, you can go one way. But if you have nothing at all—absolutely nothing at all—and nowhere to get anything, then you go another.'

He had thought that there was something in what she said, and yet he had not quite agreed with her. There would have been no end to the consequences of whole-hearted agreement.

He soon stopped asking intimate questions, because he knew that it was a mistake to be too curious about people who drift into your life and must soon inevitably drift out again. That wasn't the way to live.

The secret of life was never to go too far or too deep. And so you left these people alone. They would be pretty certain to tell you lies, anyhow. And they had their own ways of getting along, don't you worry.(26)

It is this element of self-preservation which he sees so woefully absent in Julia: 'And it was against Mr Mackenzie's code to believe that any female existed without a sense of self-preservation.'(27) Mackenzie recalls how she began to depress him and finally 'a feeling of caution and suspicion which almost amounted to hatred had entirely overcome him'.(28) Even Mackenzie's hatred seems passionless, for it emerges out of a need to retreat from human contact after his sexual drive has spent itself. He is unable to look upon the woman arousing his lust as any more than an object. The female is flesh, a source of a biological conclusion; a more complex relationship demands giving, caring, and other human virtues which Mackenzie does not have. These virtues remain forever outside his 'code' which protects him, but ultimately cuts him off from the vitality of human feeling.

This characterisation of Mackenzie is not weakened by its obviousness and bitter edge, because the dramatic confrontation between the two of them which follows brings Mackenzie much closer to us, as we see him for the pathetic figure he is, afraid to engage the world in any real way. At the end of the novel, when he and Julia meet again, we know that he is a man who must continually create false illusions out of his hollow existence. Julia hasn't the strength to change her life, but Mackenzie no longer has even an idea of how to change his. Ironically enough, the insincerity and cruelty of the Mackenzies of the world generate Julia's strength: something Macenzie recognises, though without concommitant recognition of the reflection on himself. And Julia is well aware of this irony:

'Of course, you clung on because you were obstinate. You clung on because people tried to shove you off, despised you, and were rude to you. So you clung on. Left quite alone, you would have let go of your own accord.'(180)

In the novel's final scene Mackenzie and Julia run into each other on the street in Paris. The narrator's irony is decisive: Mackenzie decides to speak to Julia, 'the romantic side of his nature asserted itself'.(190) As he sits with her in the café, he thinks to himself, '"I'm not a bad sort . . ."'(190) He looks Julia over carefully, sees her attractiveness fading and a 'feeling of melancholy crept over him'.(191) But it's too late for Julia to appeal to guilt or romantic feelings on his part; she embarrasses and frightens him by putting the whole affair on the grounds where he established it. She abruptly asks him for 100 francs. He passes her some money and just as abruptly leaves, and as he does he is not even dimly aware that she has at last exacted a price for his erotic experience, and he is only left with the memory of, in Simone de Beauvoir's words, 'the lonely satisfaction of the orgasm', which after all is his only capability anyway.

An even more detailed analysis of masculine attitudes toward the female is presented in the character of Horsfield. He first encounters Julia when he sees her strike Mackenzie in the restaurant, and follows her outside. Their meeting begins in ironic circumstances; it is almost as though he is poised to begin where Mackenzie left off. At first the signals for the reader to be certain of the outcome would indicate that Horsfield is merely a younger, perhaps more adventurous Mackenzie, and the whole process of masculine possession of Julia is to begin over again. But it is not so simple; Horsfield's false starts, his widely varying reactions, his own conflicting emotions—all of these elements are too well portrayed. Horsfield is much more at the centre of the novel than Mackenzie as a character; and, as the title suggests, we are concerned with Julia 'after' Mr Mackenzie. Mackenzie is the most potent outside force upon Julia in the novel, but Horsfield is a more fully drawn character.

Several circumstances in her own life probably gave Rhys the confidence to study more deeply masculine motivation and desire directed toward the female. By this time she and Leslie Tilden Smith were living together. The name 'Horsfield' was suggested by Smith, and was the name of a friend of his who had been killed in World War I. The character was in large part drawn from Tilden Smith himself. The house described where Horsfield lives in Holland Park, 'five rooms over a stable', fits the description of the converted carriage house where Rhys and Tilden Smith lived at 1 Boyne Terrace Mews, Holland Park. Horsfield's cat, Jones, was probably Jonathan, Tilden Smith's cat. The point is not to identify absolutely these sources with the characters and places in the work, but to suggest that Rhy's own experience, from which she almost exclusively drew, had broadened her perceptions and insights, and that her life with Tilden Smith helped her to create a more rounded and complex male character.

George Horsfield, unlike Mackenzie, is a young man in quest of a 'humanity in which he felt he was lamentably deficient'.(36) He is alert to the openly sensual; he watches two women as they pass by him on the street: 'they flaunted their legs and breasts as if they were glad to be alive'. (36) But beneath his buoyancy and seeming zest for experience, he also catches 'a sweet sadness like a hovering ghost',(37) in the air. His contrasting perceptions are recorded in quick juxtapositions which reveal his abrupt vacillations within that romantic mixture of expectation and melancholy. Even before he meets Julia we see in him an unstable mixture of emotions and widely contrasting feelings that could bring disaster to any relationship beyond the casually sexual encounter which he seems initially to want with Julia. But his emotions are in such riot that he, unlike Mackenzie, is not sure just what kind of relationship he does want.

With a sure stroke of narrative skill the preliminary scenes and the early meeting with Julia are rendered from Horsfield's point of view. As might be expected, Julia is far too complex and remote a figure for Horsfield to understand. During their first meeting he justifies her rudeness as a result of the harshness of her life and is left very much at a loss as to his own feelings. He is simply unprepared for any reactions on her part which do not support his romantic projection of himself in search of his humanity. When he takes her to a film on their first evening of their meeting, Julia begins to cry and Horsfield immediately disengages himself from her emotionally: 'he felt that her sorrows were nothing whatever to do with him. On the contrary, he was the injured party.'(44) He is both embarrassed and amazed and admits to himself that 'all he wanted to do was have a good time and not think'.(45) His search for humanity is, in fact, a quest for sensual experience. But he knows that human feeling is not offered without cost and even the instinct of pity, if allowed to 'degenerate from the general to the particular', could make life become 'completely impossible'.(46) But he pursues the possibility of the impossible.

At their first meeting he brings Julia back to his hotel room, she tells him about returning Mackenzie's 1,500 francs, and he replaces the money. This gesture, however, is not symbolic of Horsfield's having replaced Mackenzie, but it does bring out in him the worst of masculine emotions, for 'when he had done this he felt powerful and dominant. Happy. He smiled at Julia rather foolishly.'(47) But Julia's calm acceptance proves anti-climatic and leaves him embarrassed. Horsfield has not yet developed the insulated hardness of his predecessor in Julia's life, and he recognises in her indifference 'a sort of hard-won courage'. After their long conversation during this first evening, in which Julia gets drunk and tells him of her past and of Mackenzie, Horsfield has achieved part of the point of his quest that he left England and came to France for in the first place; he is 'filled with a glow of warm humanity. . . . "Hang it all, one can't leave this unfortunate creature alone to go and drink herself dotty."'(54) He gives Julia his address in London, and his 'quest for humanity' is temporarily satisfied. He feels good; his romantic illusions are left intact. He has helped someone. But, as events will make clear to young Horsfield, humanity comes at a higher price.

The point of view controls what might otherwise be a prosaic if not merely melodramatic relationship between Horsfield and Julia. During their first meeting it is rendered exclusively through Horsfield's reactions to Julia, and the narrator satirically reveals his motivations and intellectual juggling. His footwork is quite humorous at times as he bounces back and forth between caution and recklessness, attraction and revulsion for Julia. But for their second meeting the narrator moves the focus back and forth between both of them in order to catch the by-play and parrying beyond the dialogue. The shift within the consciousness of the two is effective here as it was not in *Quartet*, where Heidler, for example, was not convincing as a character because the narrator could not free herself from Marya's point of view. This failure in *Quartet* nearly reduced the novel to melodrama. But the shifting point of view in *Mr Mackenzie* not only accommodates the unfolding of a relationship, it inaugurates and sustains the entire dramatic situation.

During their first meeting in London, we initially see a change in Horsfield. He is more distant and under control, but more interested: 'The suggestion of age and weariness in her face fascinated Mr Horsfield.'(91) At the same time as his romantic illusions ebb, there is an increasingly erotic attraction and feeling of intimacy, 'and he hated the feeling of intimacy. It made something in him shrink back and long to escape.' (90) Although he does not know it yet, he is far more driven to Julia sexually than he admits or even understands. When he takes her to her cheap hotel in Bloomsbury, he feels her 'leaning very close to him'. As the taxi stops suddenly she is thrown against him and 'her body felt soft and yielding'.(93)

When they meet again Julia has attended the death-bed and funeral of her mother and endured the final break-up with her sister Norah. Horsfield's indecisiveness is clear; he had just cancelled their date for dinner, but he comes around to her hotel after all and catches up with her as she walks along the street. Julia is near despair when Horsfield arrives, and her odd subsequent behaviour alerts him to her mood, while he is also put off physically:

> Her body looked abandoned when she danced, but not voluptuously so. It was the abandonment of fatigue.
> Mr Horsfield lowered his eyes moodily so that as Julia and her partner passed his table he saw only her legs, appearing rather too plump in flesh-coloured stockings. She seemed to him to be moving stiffly and rather jerkily. It was like watching a clockwork toy that has nearly run down.(148)

For Julia the game is temporarily over; her defences are completely down. It is no longer a matter of offering a soft and pliant body, which she has learned to do so well. At this moment she desperately needs some recognition of her affinity to the human race. Her need is not sexual; it is human. As Horsfield starts to leave her at the hotel she says, '"You mustn't leave me. Don't leave me. You must stay with me. Please."'(149) He does. He puts his hand on her arm, and feels her shivering: 'This added to his sensation of excitement and triumph.'(150) It is indeed triumphantly that he contemplates his good fortune. This is the imagined ideal situation in which the male can indulge and respect himself. He satisfies his sexual urge and maintains his self-image as the gallant protector.

But it once again dawns upon Horsfield that it is not a perfect world, one where we can act out our romantic illusions without losing them. Julia's body is 'soft and unresisting', but Horsfield recognises the incompleteness of the act, the lack of any communiation, only the animal satisfactions:

> 'You are thirsty, dried up with thirst, and yet you don't know it until somebody holds up water to your mouth and says: "You're thirsty, drink." It's like that. You are thirsty, and you drink.

'And then you wonder all sorts of things, discontendly and disconnectedly.

'"But the worst of it is," he thought, "that one can never know what the woman is really feeling."'(153)

After he has entered her and is spent, he dresses and leaves before she awakens, and as he closes the door behind him 'he felt an enormous relief'.(155)

For Julia the whole relationship is nothing. When she awakens the next morning to read Horsfield's note, it is 'as if she were reading something written by a stranger to someone she had never seen'.(157) Julia no longer has either capacity or will to connect or build upon human relationships. Either she recognises with keen perception that the Horsfields of the world, in spite of their good intentions, will never commit themselves deeply to her, or she simply no longer cares. It is probably a little of both. After Mr Mackenzie she is going to avoid the hurt of the inevitable outcome of another relationship with a male, but she knows deeply that there are those moments of loneliness when she needs temporarily the warmth and proximity of another human being even if it is a male, who in spite of his subterfuges only wants to possess her. The language of sex fails here, for possession is not an accurate word; sexual intercourse in this instance is hardly possession.

The outcome of this affair has become predictable and even inevitable. But through this fleeting relationship we have learned a great deal about both characters and, more important, about human capacity and need. Julia's initial reactions after having slept with Horsfield for the first time are almost misleading, for beneath her resigned and distant façade there is a person always on the brink of hysteria. The next time they meet Horsfield follows her up the stairs to her room in the dark. Suddenly she shouts out and becomes hysterical, imagining that a stranger has approached her in the dark. This scene verges on farce, but we have learned that farcical or comic scenes in Rhys's novels are frequently the blackest.

In one of the most poignant scenes in the novel, Julia is packing for her return to Paris and she shows Horsfield the letter she has received from her first lover, Mr James. She tells Horsfield how she felt about him:

He was a sort of god to me and everything he did was right. Isn't one a fool when one's a kid? But sometimes I used to pray that he'd

lose all his money, because I imagined that if that happened I'd see
him oftener. And then I'd imagine myself working for him, or
somehow getting money to give him. He'd have thanked me if
he'd known what I was praying for, wouldn't he?(173)

These are the feelings of a woman in love, the same feelings that Anna
Morgan had for Walter Jeffries but was unable to express. The break
up of this first love was far more devastating than leaving Mr
Mackenzie, and far more revealing. It was this blow from which Julia
has never recovered, for the outcome of the early affair shaped and
formed her attitude toward men, and made her suspicious of all
human relationships—destroyed her will.

There is an awful knowledge that comes to Horsfield out of the
brief affair between Julia and himself. It has taught him that self-
protection is the rule of the jungle: the Julias of the world only pull
you down; buy yourself sex and, if you want, find a woman who has
not been ravaged and will help you to preserve your male illusions,
one whom you also can domesticate. After Julia has returned to Paris,
Horsfield writes that he will not be able to turn up as soon as he had
thought, but he encloses two five pound notes, a cheap price to pay in
case he might be lonely in Paris. He has learned, and to learn this is to
lose something greater.

Besides Julia's two abortive relationships with Mackenzie and
Horsfield, there is a third, with her sister, which also comes to a bitter
end. The contrast drawn between Julia and her sister, Norah, is an
important one. Norah represents the woman who played it straight
and took no risks, who accepted her lower-middle-class life in all its
drabness; she is among life's defeated women. Beneath her grim
stoicism lurks an embittered, self-pitying woman. The narrator's
opening description characterises her:

> Her head and arms drooped as she sat. She was pale, her colourless
> lips pressed tightly together into an expression of endurance. She
> seemed tired.
>   Her eyes were like Julia's, long and soft. Fine wrinkles were
> already forming in the corners. She wore a pale green dress with a
> red flower fixed in the lapel of the collar. But the dress had lost its
> freshness, so that the flower looked pathetic.(71)

We learn from her 'cold' face that 'warmth and tenderness were dead
in her'.(71) In spite of this hardness Julia seeks some acknowledgment

of their relationship, even a remote family recognition. Julia longs 'for some show of affection . . . but Norah kept looking at her as if she were something out of a zoo'.(73) Julia is rebuffed and feels only an 'answering indifference' coming from Norah.

Norah has been beaten down in a way very different, but the same social and economic forces have worked upon her. She is a woman with middle-class tastes 'left without the money to gratify them . . . yet holding desperately to both her tastes and opinions'.(74) Out of these values she has formed, she rebukes Julia for her shiftlessness, her conduct with men, her failure to care for her dying mother. The most frequent word Julia uses to characterise her is 'fierce', and this is a fierceness created out of hatred and self-pity.

The difference between the two is fundamental. Norah's resentment and hatred incapacitate her. She is no longer able to feel anything except bitterness. Caring for her dying mother kept her self-pity alive, and after her mother's death she will resign herself to living under the cold comfort and care of Miss Wyatt, a middle-aged woman whose 'hair was cut very short' and who 'wore a coat and skirt of grey flannel, a shirt blouse, and a tie'.(95) Julia's fundamental outlook is set in careful contrast to Norah's; Julia is vulnerable where Norah is hard, but because she is able to retain some feeling in spite of her constant adversity and unwise adventures, Julia elicits our sympathy. She recognises Norah's defeat in Norah's coldness and self-righteous moral superiority. Norah's indifference to her awakens a forceful if temporary determination in Julia that has never been evoked when she has been let down by a man:

> She had lost the feeling of indifference to her fate, which in Paris had sustained her for so long. She knew herself ready to struggle and twist and turn, to be unscrupulous and cunning as are all weak creatures fighting for their lives against the strong.(77)

It has been pointed out several times that the heroine in Rhys's novels fares no better in her relationships with women than she does with men. Just as Anna Morgan was exploited as much by women as men, so too is Julia. There are, however, those rare and fleeting moments when we see this yearning among the heroines for feminine companionship, apparent through the loneliness created by its absence. Infrequent recognition of feminine affinity usually occurs in passages following a crisis and is marked by a frank sensuality; in fact, they are more sensual than any passage which describes men. No male—female sexual act is ever described in any detail in Rhys's fiction, and in them, where the woman is always passive, there is an absence of sensuality. It is quite the opposite in those passages where the heroine recognises sexuality in another woman. The first of these occurs in the short story 'Vienne' when Francine and Pierre are fleeing across middle Europe and stop at an inn. Francoise sees a young woman working at the inn and watches her carrying pails and tubs.

> She wore a white bodice so thin that one could plainly see the shape of her breasts, a dark skirt, her feet were bare, her head was small, set on a very long neck, her eyes slanted like Ishima's—I watched her with an extraordinary pleasure because she was so slim and young and finely drawn. And because I imagined that when she glanced at me her eyes had the expression of some proud, wild thing—say a young lioness—instead of the usual stupid antagonism of one female looking at another. (245)

This is indeed a rare moment when one woman openly responds to another without antagonism. There is a kind of purity in this response to a member of her own sex which we never find between males and females in Rhys's novels. Men and women are so unsure of their sexual roles in the tarnished male—female encounters that there is an utter absence of physical pleasure; both seem incapable of response.

Toward the end of *Mr Mackenzie*, after Julia has returned to Paris, she goes to a café for a *fine*. 'It was a low-down place', but Julia sees a beautiful woman behind the counter:

> . . . her voice was very soft and her eyes were big and dark. She was a slim woman with full, soft breasts.
>
> Julia had a great longing to go up to the woman and talk to her. It was rum; some people did look like that—not cruel, but kind and soft. One in a million looked like that.
>
> She sat thinking: 'If I could talk to her, if only I could go up and tell her all about myself and why I am unhappy, everything would be different afterwards.' (184)

Although rare, brief, and distant, these scenes carefully contrast with the sordid passing encounters in the streets and hotel rooms with men. They recall with a passion something betrayed between women—an intimacy no longer a part of the feminine consciousness.

After Leaving Mr Mackenzie is a novel intimately concerned on every level with the nature of human relationships, the ambivalence and questions of truth and reality, lies and illusions, that exist for both sexes. The novel organises itself on the motivations and cross-purposes of the characters within the framework of these questions. These are the considerations which force themselves on the imaginations of the characters and, consequently, upon us as readers. The movement of the novel traces with shattering accuracy the desires and self-induced illusions of the male. It makes poignantly visible the male role in the sexual power struggle in which he must not only dominate but justify domination to himself. The results of this domination for the female are also made very plain. The social and economic order is all on the side of the male, and in widely different ways makes victims of both Julia and Norah.

Overlying this entire exploration at all stages is the figure of Julia Martin, who stands as the female victim in all the games projected by the male to satisfy and preserve his vanity. Her struggle can also be seen as an elaborated image of human isolation on every level. All four figures in the novel are isolated; in each we see the impulse toward human companionship; and, on the part of the men, the price they are unwilling to pay. In the end Julia, Norah, Mackenzie, and Horsfield are already too unwilling, incapable, or, in Julia's case, too broken down to find any meaningful human bond; the barriers erected by their private selves, in different ways and for different reasons, are too painfully strong. Each is fixed, either by choice or circumstance, in a world whose highest value is protection, not love. And the metaphysical weight of the novel exposes the vacuity of this hierarchy.

5 Good Morning, Midnight

In the 1930s more than any other decade of this century English writers exaggerated the moral, social, and realistic content of art. Among the many important observations that Samuel Hynes makes in his excellent study of the decade, *The Auden Generation*,[1] is the fact that the major writers of the period who took up the social and political causes were from the middle class, most of them came from professional families, and were educated at Oxford and Cambridge. In spite of the fact that Rhys wrote precisely of what it was like to be down and out in both Paris and London, her fiction was not a literature of social engagement. Even by 1939 her writing seemed untouched by the devastating political and military events which had occurred and the even more horrendous ones which were on the horizon. A passing reference in *Good Morning, Midnight* to Franco's Spain and the fact that it is October, 1937, are the only indications that the outside world has changed very much since Marya Zelli first came to Paris in the aftermath of World War I. Set against the 1930s writing of Graham Greene, George Orwell and nearly every other English prose writer of the period, with the exception in a very different way of Henry Green, her work continued to rest on the power of style rather than new subject matter, intuition rather than analysis, the private rather than the public self.

Throughout the thirties Rhys's heroines saw the world from the inside rather than the outside. Her aim was the perfection of rendering private consciousness through style, not the achievement of an enlarged vision of the contemporary world. *Good Morning, Midnight* advanced the major themes of her earlier work and deepened her portrait of women's emotional life. Published at the very end of this period, as the Germans were advancing on Poland, the novel brought to a close a sustained melancholy picture of a small part of human life during the 1920s and 1930s. Although there is little sense of historical period in the work, *Good Morning, Midnight*, in an uncanny way that is felt by the reader rather than directly experienced by the characters, portrays the broad economic decline and the sense of impending disaster that was a part of the 1930s. For example, there is an enormous emphasis in this novel on how much things cost, how much money one needs, how much protection money affords. Set as it is in Paris, the novel also brings Rhys's fiction full circle, and it confirms in another way that her real literary affinities are French rather than English.

Sasha Jansen bears the cumulative burdens of Rhys's earlier heroines; she is Julia Martin grown older, a bit more out of control, but for the present at least, less financially desperate. The cards, however, are out on the table for Sasha; it takes more alcohol, more luminal for her to keep things in place. The arrangement of the room, the meals in cafés, the *fine* in a bar, the buying of a hat, all define the nature of her attempts at self-control—they have become rituals, substitutes for meaning in a life that seems without purpose. They form a geometry of movement which leads nowhere, but charts for her a course to preserve some semblance of sanity.

> I stayed there, staring at myself in the glass. What do I want to cry about? . . . On the contrary, it's when I am quite sane like this, when I have had a couple of extra drinks and am quite sane, that I realize how lucky I am. Saved, rescued, fished-up, half-drowned, out of the deep, dark river, dry clothes, hair shampooed and set. Nobody would know I had ever been in it. Except, of course, that there always remains something. Yes, there always remains something. . . . Never mind, here I am, sane and dry, with my place to hide in. What more do I want? . . . I'm a bit of an automaton, but sane surely—dry, cold and sane. Now I have forgotten about dark streets, dark rivers, the pain, the struggle and the drowning . . . . (10)

The passage above reveals the novel's central metaphor. Moreover, it traces the outlines of Sasha's life and hints at the central structural design of the novel. The reference to drowning and water set up a psychological pattern of sexual violation and fear which gradually reveal the depth of the heroine's consciousness and the entire range of her personality and feeling. This trope reflects Sasha's essential view of life in a world in which all her actions and reactions seem attempts to master the threats that such a world imposes. The opening line of the passage is the initial clue to the obsessional consciousness that the novel will explore.

Sasha is a veteran, however; she knows the boundaries: 'The thing is to have a programme, not to leave anything to chance—no gaps.'(15) She has come to Paris for a short visit, paid for by a woman friend who thinks she needs a change. Her return to Paris is like encountering an old lover: 'Paris is looking very nice tonight. . . . You are looking very nice tonight, my beautiful, my darling, and oh what a bitch you can be! But you didn't kill me after all, did you? And they couldn't kill me either.'(16) But also, like an old lover it can stir memories and make one vulnerable again. *Good Morning, Midnight* is a novel where present and past collide, and the past is a dark and looming shadow over the present until the very end.

The major portion of Part I carefully develops Sasha's earlier memories of her Paris failures. The first is her recollection of a scene in a dress shop where she had worked. The owner 'Mr Blank' from England visits the shop and she immediately feels fearful and threatened. She is called in to deliver a message which he is still writing and her paranoia mounts: 'He is, he is. He's doing it on purpose. I know it. I feel it.'(24) She is vulnerable and unprotected. 'Mr Blank' becomes the archetype of all those forces which hold her hostage:

> Well, let's argue this out, Mr Blank. You, who represent Society, have the right to pay me four hundred francs a month. That's my market value, for I am an inefficient member of Society, slow in the uptake, uncertain, slightly damaged in the fray, there's no denying it. So you have the right to pay me four hundred francs a month, to lodge me in a small, dark room, to clothe me shabbily, to harass me with worry and monotony and unsatisfied longings till you get me to the point when I blush at a look, cry at a word. We can't all be happy, we can't all be rich, we can't all be lucky— and it would be so much less fun if we were. Isn't it so, Mr Blank? (29)

The malignancy of the faceless and nameless oppressor is seen more clearly by Sasha than by any of Rhys's other heroines. From this combination of paranoia and insight, Sasha recognises those forces in society which turn her into a weak and helpless figure who simply cannot get on. It is in this condition that women like her turn to men for protection and in so doing leave themselves subject to the forces which crush them. Nor is there a way to retreat, for 'the passages will never lead anywhere, the doors will always be shut. I know.'(31)

These scenes from her earlier memories of Paris are very skillfully
drawn to reveal in precise terms the formation of Sasha's attitudes and
fears. They are important to our understanding of her later behaviour
and anxieties as the plot of the novel unfolds.

We learn gradually how important the ritualised programme
which she has adopted for her present visit is to her, and how flimsy its
protection. At one point she enters a restaurant for a ritual meal, but as
she eats with her eyes glued to the plate she imagines 'everybody in
the room is staring at me; all the eyes in the room are fixed on me'.
(50) Even the architecture takes on an ominous, haunting quality:
'Walking in the night with the dark houses over you, like
monsters.'(32) The grotesque imagery and Sasha's psychological
reactions are similar to the image of 'Mr Blank': 'If you have money
and friends, houses are just houses with steps and a front door—
friendly houses where the door opens and somebody meets you,
smiling . . . .', but if you are a 'poor devil without any friends and
without any money. Then they step forward, the waiting houses, to
frown and crush.'(32) This image of the enclosing streets is a
frequently recurring one in Rhys's novels and beyond its paranoidal
obsessional quality it accommodates the consciousness of the heroine,
the way in which she constructs her apprehension of the external
world. Her world is hotel rooms, streets, cafés, and the images which
emerge are gathered up in the narration and the style, creating a
rhythm that accretes meaning as the images form a barometer to the
heroine's psychological condition.

Because *Good Morning, Midnight* is rendered entirely through
Sasha's consciousness in first person narration except for dialogue, her
psychological states are necessarily well controlled by the style. The
style not only reflects her various immediate states of mind, but as it
orders her consciousness in language it offers further clues to the
deeper, inner self. The brutally understated style gives penetrating
focus to Sasha's dreams and the imagery, with its sustained and
continued tropes, amplifies and expands meaning beyond the
immediate rendering of consciousness.

The style also accommodates a vision of life that the initial
metaphor imposes: a journey through 'dark streets, dark rivers, the
struggle and the drowning . . .'. (10) And this image leads to the
inevitable vortex:

It doesn't matter, there I am, like one of those straws which floats
round the edge of a whirlpool and is gradually sucked into the

centre, the dead centre, where everything is stagnant, everything is calm. (44)

In the image of the whirlpool is the denial of the self. Having been swept down by the movement of life and finally engulfed by its vortex, the conscious self at this point, like a Beckett character, is apparently left shapeless—without form. But Sasha somehow, more like a Pirandello hero, survives, and *Good Morning, Midnight* traces this tenuous line of survival out from the vortex. Ultimately, however, the novel upholds Beckett's view that memory is useless, which the images themselves emanating from Sasha's consciousness bear out. As these images gather force through the novel they will add resonance to its theme.

What proves to be the most significant encounter in the novel occurs near the close of Part I, when Sasha meets a man on the street as she is leaving a bar. She immediately recognises him as a poor gigolo and starts to send him away, but she thinks, 'this is where I might be able to get some of my own back. You talk to them, you pretend to sympathise; then just at the moment when they are not expecting it, you say: "Go to hell."'(72) The gigolo's name is René, but his name is only given once and Sasha constantly refers to him as 'the gigolo' which is indicative of her sense of the relationship. Moreover, Sasha's own name is rarely referred to; there is a nameless quality to both characters which reinforces the dissolution of self, central to the theme of the novel. The gigolo has a curious appeal for her from the first, and in spite of all her hurt at the hands of men he momentarily touches her. He tells her that he has approached her because she looks kind and 'won't betray' him, and Sasha thinks, 'Now it won't be so easy.'(73) The beginning of this relationship is the turning point of the novel. In spite of her professed hatred for men, Sasha's growing interest in René should not surprise us, for the dominant energies in Rhys's novels have always been on the side of the underdog. The gigolo is charming, hopeful, and, of course, clever. He tells Sasha at their first meeting:

'But it isn't money I want,' he says. 'Really it isn't money. What I hoped was that we could go somewhere where we could be quite alone. I want to put my head on your breast and put my arms round you and tell you everything. You know, it's strange, but that's how I feel tonight. I could die for that—a woman who would put her arms round me and to whom I could tell everything. Couldn't we go somewhere like that?'(75–6)

Sasha is not swayed by this, she has heard it too many times and is aware of René's charming insincerity. His appeal is to the maternal, for he knows that in this role women are the least ambivalent. Sasha continues on with him throughout the evening, listening to his hopeful schemes, and thinking that it is harmless for her. 'He is out for money and I haven't got any. I am invulnerable.'(76) Besides the obvious reversal of the male–female roles that Sasha is enjoying, lines such as the above form a careful contrast to the scene between Sasha and 'Mr Blank' where she felt vulnerable before he had set eyes on her. As she listens to René go on and on, she identifies with him, and, recognising he is in some sort of trouble, wants to 'comfort him' or 'cheer him up'. She believes none of his story, however, and when he asks her to sleep with him that night she refuses. But having done so there is a flicker of regret; she knows she can fall again into the world of the self that closes everything else out. 'I'll lie in bed all day, pull the curtains and shut the damn world out.'(81)

The brief encounter with René results in a subtle, if only temporary change in Sasha. She does not shut the 'damn world out', but goes out the next day with Delmar, a Russian friend she has met who takes her to meet his friend, Serge, a painter. It is an afternoon filled with memories, and as is so frequently the case in Rhys's fiction, the memories are triggered by music. Sasha first hears a tune on the street and this recalls her encounter with a man who had tried to pick her up and whom she told she was hungry and had not eaten in three days. He immediately ran off, thinking fate had conspired against him—'what with his girl's shoes and me wanting food'.(90) When she and Delmar arrive at Serge's studio, music again triggers memories. As the old gramophone plays Martinique music, Sasha remembers a scene in a hammock with a Caribbean landscape and the song itself wails of lost love. Sasha gets a little drunk and more memories flood her consciousness, and finally the press is on. Delmar has brought her here to buy one of Serge's pictures, but it is a soft sell; the two have set the mood and Sasha buys a picture for 600 francs, and later that night as she strolls past the prostitutes, she still feels 'fairly exalted'. This entire incident dramatises with frequent irony a variety of reversals with money the common denominator. In a society where values and roles are dependent upon the economic order, Sasha finds herself, temporarily at least, sought out as a 'protector'. Her first instinct, however, is immediately correct—she is invulnerable to the deliberate ploys; they do not really touch her. To buy a dinner for René or buy a painting from Serge seems only to amuse her. She is both amused and flattered, because she sees with clarity the motivations of the male in these circumstances, for she has been in their situation. As Shulamith Firestone has written in *The Dialectic of Sex*:

> However, the woman knows that this idealization, which she works so hard to produce, is a lie, and that it is only a matter of time before he 'sees through her.' Her life is a hell, vacillating between an all-consuming need for male love and approval to raise her from her class subjection, to persistent feelings of inauthenticity when she does achieve his love. Thus her whole identity hangs in the balance of her love life. She is allowed to love herself only if a man finds her worthy of love.[2]

After Sasha meets the gigolo the style of the novel becomes more open, the sentences longer, the images less grotesque, and Sasha's thought patterns less obsessive. In short, Sasha has begun to look outside herself. She sees a shabbily dressed working girl behind a bar and in another of those rare moments of affinity between women Sasha thinks, 'I know her'. She finds herself touched:

> Sorry for her? Why should I be sorry for her? Hasn't she got sturdy legs and curly hair? And don't her strong hands sing the Marseillaise? And when the revolution comes, won't those be the hands to be kissed? Well, so Monsieur Rimbaud says, doesn't he? I hope he's right. I wonder, though, I wonder, I wonder . . . .(105)

This scene is different from similar scenes in the earlier novels; it has more dimension, for the woman is viewed in a social context. This wider range of focus, however, does not deceive someone as cynical and worldly as Sasha:

> The hands that sing the Marseillaise, the world that could be so different—what's all that to me? What can I do about it? Nothing. I deceive myself.
>   That's settled. I can start on the second Pernod.(107)

The room itself, which had become the symbol of Sasha's enclosed protective world is now: 'This damned room—it's saturated with the past.'(109)

The words above close Part II of the book and set up the long memory section which forms Part II. Part III recalls Sasha's marriage to Enno, who reminds us of Stephan Zelli in *Quartet*. It tells of their early love and hope as they come to Paris, and then the fallen hopes and the final break up. Enno tells her one day, 'you don't know how to make love . . . you're too passive, you're lazy, you bore me'.(128) He leaves but soon returns, yet things are no longer the same. A baby arrives but is stillborn. Enno leaves for good and Sasha wanders the Paris streets one after the other, and from room to room she moves:

> Eat. Drink. Walk. March. Back to the hotel. To the Hotel of Arrival, the Hotel of Departure, the Hotel of the Future, the Hotel of Martinique and the Universe. . . . Back to the hotel without a name in the street without a name. You press the button and the door opens. This is the Hotel Without-a-Name in the Street Without-a-Name, and the clients have no names, no faces. You go up the stairs. Always the same stairs, always the same room.
> The room says: 'Quite like old times. Yes? . . . No? . . . Yes.' (144–5)

It is out of this past that Sasha's present has been formed. She has wandered through that world of J. Alfred Prufrock, the 'half-deserted streets,' the 'restless nights in one night cheap hotels.' Yes, Sasha has

> . . . known them all already, known them all—
> . . . known the evenings, morning, afternoons,

It is this paranoid, obsessive world similar to Prufrock's from which Sasha has emerged not quite whole. And like Prufrock, past experience has made it necessary to 'prepare a face' for survival in the present.

As the novel reaches its dramatic close in Part IV, we become increasingly aware that Sasha's is an almost archetypal journey of return. It begins as an attempt to face the past by revisiting it in a most cautious way, but despite the caution it floods up and nearly engulfs the present. Sasha, however, is gradually able to overcome its movement. Through a series of ironic reversals she will be able at last to greet it in all of its blackness, as the novel's title suggests.

René, for all his pretense and deviousness, has a profound effect upon Sasha. Although she sees through him she is warmed—touched, because he sees her as a human being. Sasha knows she has very little for him to exploit and she feels safe; yet she is vulnerable to his charm. She had thought she was safe because she had measured all male–female relationships in terms of money, having long forgotten or abandoned the prospect of a relationship based on deeper human feelings. When he tells her she brings him luck, she thinks to herself, 'Well, I've never thought of myself in that way before.'(152), but when he takes her hand and looks at her ring she tells him, ' "No good. Only worth about fifty francs—if that." '(152) She knows him well, but as she walks away she is excited, as well as agitated. As she thinks about her present state the prose turns to the language of the novel's central metaphor:

> And, after all, the agitation is only on the surface. Underneath I'm indifferent. Underneath there is always stagnant water, calm, indifferent—the bitter peace that is very near to death, to hate. . . . (153)

But René's presence begins to touch her more deeply, and although she retains her caution and builds no illusions, her 'indifference' begins to evaporate. This relationship between a knowing and mistrustful woman who has always come out on the losing end and the young gigolo whose designs and motives grow increasingly more complicated is one of growing complexity as each begins to probe more deeply and respond to the personality of the other. This is not a novel about a past innocence recaptured, but about those short and fleeting moments even in the worst of lives that touch one occasionally.

By implication the novel also speaks of release and liberation. Temporarily free of economic oppression, Sasha is able to be with a male and establish a relationship outside of the usual patronage system. With René she need not give her feelings inauthentically in exchange for security. Part of the eventual terror which she is to feel comes out of the fact that with René she can be emotionally sincere in her female role, and this for a woman, especially a woman such as Sasha, is alien, for a life-time of conditioning has pulled her to the opposite pole. It would be inaccurate to overstress this point, because the novel does not allude to this drastic change in roles with any specificity, nor does it elaborate upon its conditions, but we are able to see clearly enough the implications of this brief shift in roles between the male and the female and its effect upon the heroine.

Because of their nature, these brief encounters with René gradually bring Sasha out of herself. She sees René as a person who lives in the future, who has not yet been beaten down, a creature of hope who will live by his wits. René plans to go to England where the women with money will long for him, but Sasha contrasts his hopes with the reality of England. She knows. Yet we see the change in Sasha as she talks to René. Her thoughts and comments take on a rhetorical sharpness as she comes out of herself. The style in its directness also reveals the change which is taking place inside her. As she tells René about England she thinks, 'We have our ration of rose-leaves, but only because rose-leaves are a gentle laxative.' She tells him, ' "You take care. You'll probably get a cigarette case en toc with your initials on it after a lot of hard work." ' (157) She is cynical and even bitter, and her view of the world has, of course, not changed, but she is out in it now, engaged temporarily. René's gaiety and ebullience have lifted her out of herself. What we begin to see here as Sasha becomes witty, charming, clever, and sarcastic, is a creature who has always had these qualities but has never had the opportunity to reveal them. This transformation is one of the novel's most important elements and the narrative skill with which it is executed is a brilliant achievement.

Sasha takes René to see the Exhibition and she explains the Star of Peace to him; she feels a bit like a schoolmistress, but she sees him shivering, for he doesn't have an overcoat. She tells him to have his rich American buy him one, but he wants to have one tailored in England. This conversation characterises René's dreamy expectations, and Sasha sees her younger self in him. They go to the Deux Magots for brandy and the atmosphere prompts a warm exchange of humorous memories. Sasha's recollections are in wide contrast to her dark memories earlier in the novel. During the exchange they discover that their adventures have coincided; they knew the same person and stayed in the same house. This coincidence brings Sasha up short; it is an intrusion. She feels more guarded and less adventuresome with René. The mutual link puts her on her guard.

And René probes deeply. This is the first time in a Rhys novel a man discusses with any openness his life; even the husbands, present and past, never look upon their wives as fit partners to discuss their ambitions or their past, to say nothing of their lack of interest in knowing anything very deeply about themselves. Enno, for example, kept Sasha as a house pet and eventually left her. René's constant

questioning makes Sasha increasingly defensive, as she in turn
becomes an increasing challenge to him. René's certainty of his
powers over women, his charm, is being put to the test. Sasha has far
deeper reasons for holding herself back from him than merely to
challenge his ego. Her sense of darkness and futility well up inside her
into a realisation which excludes the possibility of hope:

> You are walking along a road peacefully. You trip. You fall into
> blackness. That's the past—or perhaps the future. And you know
> that there is no past, no future, there is only this blackness, changing
> faintly, slowly, but always the same. (172)

The acuity of this image's truth absolutely shatters Sasha. Taken
temporarily out of her passive and obsessive vortex by René, his
questions have brought her face to face with the meaning of her life.
In a flood of hysteria she finally answers him:

> 'You want to know what I'm afraid of? All right, I'll tell
> you . . . . I'm afraid of men—yes, I'm very much afraid of men.
> And I'm even more afraid of women. And I'm very much afraid of
> the whole bloody human race. . . . Afraid of them?' I say. 'Of
> course I'm afraid of them. Who wouldn't be afraid of a pack of
> damned hyenas?' (172–3)

She rages on, telling him she only wishes she ' "had the guts to kill
[herself]" '.(173) At last, spent, she sees her 'illusion' crushed by the
whole image of her life, past and present. She feels once again she is
'lying in a misery of utter darkness'.(173) Her whole experience with
René is summed up in two sentences: 'I heave myself out of the
darkness slowly, painfully. And there I am, and there he is, the poor
gigolo.'(173)

The most striking feature of this entire scene is its economy of detail
and the precision with which Sasha's whole life comes before her. The
style acts to modulate every emotional phase which she goes through
and the reflexive quality of the images deepen our understanding of
Sasha's despair.

Even after this stream of emotion and dark conflict is revealed to
him, René remains relentless. He tells of his own wounds and asks for
pity. The context makes his appeal humorous and Sasha is rightly
flabbergasted. 'They are without mercy', she says to herself. But

René is asking for her, if only temporarily; he is appealing to all of her instincts and vanity which have lain so deeply buried, and their exposure is too much for her to handle. She wants 'out of this dream'. René's more immediate intentions emerge when he asks Julia: '"Why shouldn't we believe each other just for tonight? Will you believe something I'm going to say to you now? I want absolutely to make love to you."'(174–5) When Sasha refuses he asks her what has made her like this, and she tells him, '"it wasn't one thing. It took years. It was a slow process."' (175) But the resurrection of these vague romantic yearnings of the past is perilous for Sasha and it results in a profoundly complicated turmoil in which her whole identity seems to give way. Shadow-boxing with all of the gigolo's intense questions is the motive of seduction—Sasha's aged bitterness does not protect her from the vulnerability of the past. René is appealing to her sexual and romantic urges which have long been dormant. This is a world she has long given up; you went to bed for men's protection; you were a pet. The erotic spark has been reignited by this young gigolo. Sasha is too wise not to see through his manipulative technique and the rampant male ego which produces it, but she cannot deny its excitement—somehow it makes her alive and hopeful in a way she has not been for years.

The last section of the novel is a blur between dream and reality, hallucination and confrontation. The style never loses its sharp clarity but in places it mounts to a lyric level as Sasha's mind absorbs a confusion of what she wants to believe and what is actually happening. This scene is not at all like those scenes we remember in earlier novels where the heroine lies filled with alcohol or drugs between wakefulness and sleep, hiding in fear. This is a scene of joy and terror and, equally important, the heroine is anything but passive. Sasha has reached an emotional pitch which exposes her to the point that she can no longer assimilate the full range of her emotions.

She and René part on the street, but as she opens her door she sees him mysteriously standing in the darkness of her room, uncertain how he got there.

I have my arms round him and I begin to laugh, because I am so happy. I stand there hugging him, so terribly happy. Now everything is in my arms on this dark landing—love, youth, spring, happiness, everything I thought I had lost. I was a fool, wasn't I? to think all that was finished for me. How could it be finished?

I put up my hand and touch his hair. I've wanted to do that ever since I first saw him.(177)

René turns the light on, however, and the spell is broken. She has two drinks in spite of his admonishments and she calls the entire long evening a 'comedy'. René becomes more aggressive; they argue and thrash about on the bed. But Sasha knows this game as well as he. From this flood of passion, however, Sasha begins to feel 'uneasy' as they are about to make love; she grows 'cold and wary'. The emotional pitch remains intense for both of them, but it changes from sexual passion to mutual torture. When René forces himself on top of her, her body signals the deep riot of her conflicting feelings: 'My mouth hurts, my breasts hurt, because it hurts, when you have been dead to come alive.'(182) But Sasha knows the one vulnerable point which gives her a weapon against his physical strength; however, it is as if it were a voice from another person ('that's not me speaking') who tells René, '"You can have the money right away, so it would be a waste of time wouldn't it?"'(183) René immediately leaves, and Sasha is left in a schizophrenic state, not knowing which self she really is, the passionate woman seeking but unable to accept even a fleeting moment of human passion or the aging, lonely female who has narrowly survived the advances of a gigolo. After René leaves she huddles into a foetal position, uncertain of just which self she is:

When he has gone I turn over on my side and huddle up, making myself as small as possible, my knees almost touching my chin. I cry in the way that hurts right down, that hurts your heart and your stomach. Who is this crying? The same one who laughed on the landing, kissed him and was happy. This is me, this is myself, who is crying. The other—how do I know who the other is? She isn't me.(184)

A dialogue ensues between the two selves which brings to the surface Sasha's deepest longings and fears as well as all of the defences time and experience have taught her. Her whole life comes to the surface and cries out at the conflict between the most fundamental human instincts—to love and to protect one's self. Sasha's dialectic between selves draws the horrible conclusion that love for her is impossible. All of the betrayals and violations have left her incapable of allowing herself to feel passion again.

Sasha goes to the dressing table to see how much money the gigolo had taken and finds he only took a bit. The full dramatic impact of this discovery for Sasha is rendered on the novel's last several pages as she falls drunkenly to sleep.

The dialectic of the previous scene establishes a tragic, yet nevertheless rational, view of the tensions within the self, but the dream sequence which concludes the novel takes on a mythic quality. René's gesture defied her expectations even if it was the ultimate egocentric gesture. Sasha seeks to create, in dream, a world where Venus and Apollo are not dead. She imagines the gigolo returning, she undresses and lies in bed to await him, imagining each step he takes drawing him closer to her. As she lies there her own identity seems to be fading away. Through the open door the man in the next room who had seemed to her throughout her stay 'like the ghost of the landing'(14) enters, and as he approaches her she accepts him in lieu of René—only wanting to know whether he is wearing the white or the blue dressing gown. The tension that has been set up between Sasha and him (her subliminal interest in him, his overt interest in her, his jealous rage when René comes on the scene) culminates as he becomes a surrogate lover by coming to her as she lies there waiting for physical union: 'Then I put my arms round him and pull him down on to the bed, saying: "Yes—yes—yes . . . ."'(190)

Although so profoundly different in ways too numerous and obvious to mention, *Good Morning, Midnight* concludes on a note similar to Joyce's *Ulysses*. As the feminine consciousness releases itself in that nether world where deep truths frequently reside after a crisis between wakefulness and sleep, the self asserts a qualified affirmation—not an individual affirmation but rather an impassioned shout for the efficacy of the possibility of union between man and woman in which both natures are in harmony and love, and each fulfills the other. The context of both Sasha's and Molly Bloom's last words also includes the hopelessness of such a union because it implies a return to that prelapserian state, that ideal world before the fall. Theme and dramatic event have never been better wedded in Rhys's fiction as they have in *Good Morning, Midnight* to achieve an artistic harmony and yield such insight into the consciousness of the heroine.

Throughout this novel the reader is aware of the primary importance of style in all matters of form and expression. Its function here is beyond the conventional expectations of prose. In the heroine's movements throughout the book and in her eventual illumination the style seems to form a bi-axial movement understating, modulating, and finally overcoming the heroine's plight. The language itself becomes an extended mediation to resolve the heroine's fate. The style seems to contest the development of the novel. The architechtonics of *Good Morning, Midnight* emerge out of Sasha's obsessional preoccupations and the slender thread of events which take place during her brief visit to Paris, but it is the style which gives the full configuration of this interplay between the private consciousness and the outside world. As the style carries us through the meditations between the inner and outer self, the images found in memory, topography, and dream struggle for what seems another destiny that is finally released in the last words of the novel. As I have tried to indicate, Sasha's last words and closing gesture are no more a grand affirmation of life than Molly Bloom's. But as she opens her body to a man at the novel's end, she has at least acknowledged the need of union beyond its simple erotic dimension. Sasha's acceptance is, of course, weighted with full ironic implications, for it is in immediate recognition of the small gesture of the gigolo who did not take her money. The entire scene makes clear how tenuous and slight are the gestures that can arouse tender human feeling, especially for someone such as Sasha. Also like Molly Bloom ('give us a touch Poldy') she has learned that the smallest human contacts are what we need most, and her 'yes' is for herself as well as those who try to reach her. For Sasha, 'yes' is not necessarily an acceptance of life, but a recognition of its force. Rhys also gives vision in this conclusion to the utterly narrow and restricted choice a woman has in this world.

However we may interpret the complex reverberations at the close of *Good Morning, Midnight*, they give the book a cohesion and intricacy which is beyond Rhys's earlier novels. The loneliness of the modern experience has been drawn into the rich vortex of the feminine self and accommodated with a vitality and an understanding of human nature few novels dealing with the feminine consciousness have achieved.

Good Morning, Midnight represents a fulfillment of a loose but engaging dialectic between the self and the world that we can trace throughout Rhys's fiction. The earlier heroines fail to achieve an affirmation in their conflict with the world, but in *Good Morning, Midnight* Rhys finds in the deepest human resources a strength that confronts the terror—a strength at once fragile and human, but no longer merely defensive.

This synthesis is realised in *Good Morning, Midnight* through the character of Sasha. She is the most compelling and deeply sympathetic of Rhys's heroines. She is so, in the first place, because of her greater range of feeling and emotion. Her bitter humour and sardonic wisdom provide us with abundant clues to her deeper nature. Through Sasha we are able to see nowhere more clearly that conscious drive in Rhys's fiction to look past the awful bitterness of exclusion and defeat to a vision of sympathetic understanding and knowledge in a world of meagre opportunities and easy despair. Hers is not a vision of fleeting and private harmony of the kind that holds Mrs Ramsey together in *To The Lighthouse*, but rather one where the feminine psyche must find accommodation in the world itself. *Good Morning, Midnight* is similar to *To The Lighthouse* in that its themes and resonances reveal with clarity and force those fears which haunt the imagination, but its theme lies elsewhere, not in the passive, private world of the feminine but in an active life where human need triumphs over betrayal. There is no doubt that the women in Rhys's fiction have been crippled permanently by life, but what we also see—and no where more clearly than in *Good Morning, Midnight*—is that there is a new consciousness forming, one not formed only from anger and despair, but one imbued with an awareness that women must share equally in life's promises and defeats, and if they do not human life itself is lessened and even malformed. And this revelation is no where better expressed in Rhys's fiction than in *Good Morning, Midnight*.

6 *Wide Sargasso Sea*

Wide Sargasso Sea is both easy and difficult to place in Jean Rhys's canon. It is at once, as one critic asserts, 'a logical outgrowth of the developments in the previous four novels',[1] and quite different in treatment and subject matter, if not theme, from the four earlier novels. Rhys, of course, first used her West Indian background for material in *Voyage in the Dark*, and even in her first volume of stories explicit West Indian backgrounds are used in two of them. But the themes in *Wide Sargasso Sea* are more than an outgrowth of the earlier novels; they do, as I pointed out earlier, embody many of these same themes, but there are many subtle variations and real differences, especially in the treatment of the male personality. Her characterisation of Edward Rochester, for example, is by far the most complex and fully drawn male she has ever accomplished. *Wide Sargasso Sea* is very much a part of the Rhys canon, dealing as it does with those aspects of personality and human relationships which have always engaged her. In spite of the limitations in the character of Antoinette, the novel simultaneously deepens and, in several important ways, re-examines the nature of male and female understanding, suggesting an attitude different from her earlier novels and one especially more understanding and comprehensive of male behaviour and feeling.

Playing as it does against the background of *Jane Eyre*, *Wide Sargasso Sea* initially directs our attention to Charlotte Brontë's novel. Certainly this aspect of the novel has been the one upon which most critical discussion has fallen. Several articles have treated the novel exclusively in relation to *Jane Eyre* and the Gothic mode generally; those that have not concentrate on the West Indian background.[2] Since *Wide Sargasso Sea* deals mainly with the early life of Rochester and his mad Creole wife who lives in the attic of Thornfield Hall and finally burns it down in *Jane Eyre*, this is perhaps one reason for the novel's initial, general popularity. The exploration of the novel through its treatment of the early lives of Brontë's characters is a fruitful avenue in which to explore it, as Michael Thorpe's excellent essay makes clear, but it can also lead to a serious misunderstanding of the novel if it is not well handled.[3] For example, Dennis Porter in his essay concludes that Antoinette is a passive victim and Rochester is an example of male cruelty.[4] The whole substance and theme of *Jane Eyre* reverberate throughout *Wide Sargasso Sea*, and the reader's knowledge and understanding of *Jane Eyre* deeply enrich the experience of reading Rhys's novel. Rhys was a careful reader of *Jane Eyre* and her novel is both an appreciation and commentary upon it, but over and above this, *Wide Sargasso Sea* is an independent creation of great subtlety and skill.

David Lodge has clearly pointed out, 'it is inconceivable that *Jane Eyre* could have been written without the Romantic Movement . . . the Gothic elements constitute only a small part of Charlotte Brontë's debt to romantic literature. Far more important is the characteristically romantic theme of the novel—the struggle of an individual consciousness toward self-fulfillment—and the romantic imagery of landscape, seascape, sun, moon, and the elements through which this theme is expressed.'[5] We can make a similar observation of *Wide Sargasso Sea* and add that Rhys has not only developed these same romantic elements, she has combined them with important aspects and themes so characteristic of literary modernism, namely the emphasis on psychology, sexual motivation, and human aliena-tion. From the opening pages of the novel when the young Antoinette glimpses a vision of the lost Eden, we are placed in a nineteenth-century landscape but with all the consciousness of the more deeply hidden terrors of our own century. Rhys's material use of historical and literary background enhances her exploration of human frailty and motivation, but we are always aware that the sensibility is clearly one of contemporary understanding.

The achievement of this novel is that it engages our moral and intellectual awareness more thoroughly than do the earlier works. It does so because of its more fully balanced and amplified treatment of the male–female relationship. We recognise in this novel, as Lionel Trilling has written of *Mansfield Park*, 'an analogue with the malice of the experienced universe, with the irony of circumstance, which is always disclosing more than we bargained for'.[6] Although culture, race, nationality, all of the large categories which divide us, are thematically central to *Wide Sargasso Sea*, Rhys makes abundantly clear that it is in the exposure of our individual 'doubts' and 'hesitations', our private needs and motivations, our exposure to each other, that we discover the malice of the universe. It is out of this mutual relationship of Antoinette and Edward, of the male and the female, that Rhys's view of the self is fully expressed. The horrible vision in *Good Morning, Midnight* is somewhat released by the sympathy for and understanding of the heroine and our anger at the forces which nearly destroy her, but the anger is really without individual human focus. However, in *Wide Sargasso Sea* our release must come from our understanding of those nearly inexpressible truths which lie at the heart of all of our relationships.

The design of *Wide Sargasso Sea*, like that of all of Rhys's novels, clearly reflects her major thematic concerns; the scenes owe their symbolic quality to the thematic patterns which are crucial to the structure of the novel. We learn of the child Antoinette from the novel's opening section, and also gain a view of the insular world which emerged from childhood's impact on the interior self. Part I, besides establishing a childhood basis and pattern of experience for Antoinette's later behaviour, develops through carefully elaborated events and her reactions to them our understanding of the formation of her consciousness. By drawing attention to the cultural and historical forces and events which surround her, we are made aware of the violence, disruption, and tragedy which mark her for life. The radical social and emotional upheaval in the West Indies contained in this section provide a kind of psycho-historical background for Antoinette's life. On the novel's first page she recalls:

> Another day I heard her talking to Mr Luttrell, our neighbour and her only friend. 'Of course they have their own misfortunes. Still waiting for this compensation the English promised when the Emancipation Act was passed. Some will wait for a long time.'
> How could she know that Mr Luttrell would be the first who grew tired of waiting? One calm evening he shot his dog, swam out to sea and was gone for always. No agent came from England to look after his property—Nelson's Rest it was called—and strangers from Spanish Town rode up to gossip and discuss the tragedy.[7]

Against the background of events such as these Antoinette's childhood is spent. Emancipation could not change attitudes held for so many years, and, in fact, it released a hatred of blacks for whites that had long been suppressed:

> I never looked at any strange negro. They hated us. They called us white cockroaches. Let sleeping dogs lie. One day a little girl

followed me singing, 'Go away white cockroach, go away, go away.' I walked fast, but she walked faster. 'White cockroach, go away, go away. Nobody want you. Go away.'(23)

These images of violence and hatred are important in themselves, but, moreover, they set the pattern for Antoinette's personal outrage and terror which will follow.

Much attention could be given to the historical turmoil which so drastically affects Antoinette's early life, for it is of considerable importance to the entire social and domestic fabric of her existence; but Rhys's concentration is on the psychological, the personal traumas which historical events produce rather than on the events themselves. Of major significance is her treatment of the formation of the fears and deeply rooted feelings resulting from the slave and master, black and white relationships. The attitudes resulting from these are central to the novel's tensions. The attraction and repulsion, the sympathy and hatred, that Antoinette feels for the blacks is so basically different from Edward's comprehension of them that it epitomises the young couple's vast cultural separation. This fact is stressed again and again, and as they act out of these widely different attitudes, we are constantly made aware of the unbridgeable gulf of understanding which separates them. It is most dramatically revealed in sexual terms, as we shall see.

For all her estrangement from the native and black population, Antoinette is a part of the Islands; her attraction to the wild and the exotic confirms her affinity; it ties her irrevocably to this land, in spite of her hostility to it and it to her.

But it is a grim and dying world. In both myth and reality the whites of the Island feel as though they are in the heart of Eden after the fall. Antoinette's description of the overgrown garden on her family's decrepit estate is precise:

But it had gone wild. The paths were overgrown and a smell of dead flowers mixed with the fresh living smell. Underneath the tree ferns, tall as forest tree ferns, the light was green. Orchids flourished out of reach or for some reason not to be touched. One was snaky looking, another like an octopus with long thin brown tentacles bare of leaves hanging from a twisted root. Twice a year the octopus orchid flowered—then not an inch of tentacle showed. It was a bell-shaped mass of white, mauve, deep purples, wonderful to see. The scent was very sweet and strong. I never went near it.(19)

With the fall, of course, come desperation and violence. It is a land of deserted estates, burned houses, scorched land, overgrown roads, as though nature and man collaborated in erasing a past. Cyril Hamshere in his thorough work, *The British in the Caribbean*, cites Anthony Trollope's account of the conditions in the West Indies between 1858 and 1860, when they had reached their nadir. According to Trollope, in Roseau, Dominica, where Jean Rhys was to grow up, grass grew in the streets and Spanish Town lay half dead, 'with buildings as yellow as the fever'.[8]

And in Rhys's novel as the lush growth of nature settles over the marks of the white civilisation so, too, do the power of superstition—obeah—and other mysterious practices surface through the remnants of Christianity. When a group of blacks burn down the Coulibri Estate that Mr Mason, her mother's new husband, had restored, the family escapes only because the blacks grow fearful when the family's pet parrot is engulfed by fire and falls to the earth in a flaming mass. Antoinette recalls, 'I heard someone say something about bad luck and remembered that it was very unlucky to kill a parrot, or even to see a parrot die.'(43)

As she and her family escape to a carriage, Antoinette sees her friend, Tia, and the whole black rebellion becomes a personal betrayal as Tia hits her in the head with a stone. But in this dramatic conflict, Antoinette feels an affinity for the blacks that even the violence cannot erase: 'I looked at her and I saw her face crumble up as she began to cry. We stared at each other, blood on my face, tears on hers. It was as if I saw myself. Like in a looking-glass.'(45) In spite of the violent rupture, Antoinette remains constant in her identification with the blacks. Tia's act, however, confirms Antoinette's ultimate separation from the black culture; but she is a victim, not an agent. She will vacillate between the separate worlds of blacks and whites because in her childhood she needed both, but with the rebellion she can no longer be comfortable with both identities, a disjunction ultimately a source of her doom. She grows dependent upon both worlds but is accepted in neither. In each she will become identified with the other and be looked upon with suspicion. Furthermore, her brother's death and her mother's madness after the fire not only mark Antoinette's final separation from her childhood, they confirm her complete isolation and seal her own fate in a private schizophrenic world between two times, races, and cultures. Her mother's submission and sexual subjugation at the hands of her black caretaker is also of major significance, for it dramatises and reinforces the strong current of sexuality between the races that moves through the novel. Her mother's experiences in an admittedly different way foreshadow her own and the psycho-sexual elements are, on one level, expressive of the complicated relationships between the two races that years of slavery developed, relationships which surface in Antoinette's relationship with Edward.

The latter sections of Antoinette's narrative record the life of ritual, prayers, and order within the convent school, which becomes for her a 'refuge, a place of sunshine'.(56) She feels safe inside its walls, but her childhood illusions have apparently disappeared ('I soon forgot about happiness.'56). And the convent, although a place of sunshine, is also one 'of death'. In a lost Eden refuge, violence and death are the over-riding considerations, not happiness. This is the Antoinette whom Edward will shortly meet after the arrangements for her dowry have been made by her step-brother, Richard Mason. Her psychic legacy, shaped by the unstable mixture of two cultures, has left deep scars and abiding fears and mistrust, and her life remains filled with unfocused, uncertain passions. The concluding scenes make us aware through portents and dreams of the unstable alliances which Antoinette has made within herself and the world outside.

Part II, which takes up nearly two-thirds of the novel, is largely Edward's account of the events following his marriage to Antoinette, and it forms the narrative and thematic centre of the book. Told largely from his point of view, it records the financial arrangements prior to their wedding, the journey and arrival at Granbois, the early days of sexual passion at the doom-laden but idyllic honeymoon house, and the eventual mistrust, conflict, and sundering. There is also a short but enormously important scene between Antoinette and Christophine, the wise old native, narrated by Antoinette. Although certain elements of the Gothic mode have been earlier introduced, it is in this section that Rhys makes it an active element and combines the Gothic with pathetic fallacy to reflect Edward's rapidly changing states of being. The exotic landscape with its widely fluctuating conditions externalises his apprehension and ambivalence, as Rhys invests the lush tropics with fear, horror and malignancy along with its primitively appealing and seductive quality. At times description almost becomes incantation. The Gothic mode—besides its obvious relation to *Jane Eyre*—functions as a narrative idiom where the descriptions themselves, with their frequently elaborate portents, achieve a metaphysical relationship to the characters, not unlike the early descriptions in Conrad's *Heart of Darkness*, when the terrors of the natural world are precursive and reflective of the horror and fear of the interior self.

Although Part II is centered within Edward's intelligence, the dialogue between Antoinette and Edward is extensive and this not only expands the focus beyond Edward, who is at once cold and naïve, it dramatises the interplay of forces which work on both of them. Rhys's style in this section is triumphantly adapted to her narrative purpose. Its two qualities, which at first seem to conflict—an uncanny ability to describe an emotion completed and somehow resolved, and, at the same time a rendering of feeling as much by implication as by statement—are fused by the close relationship she draws between the natural and psychological landscape. The imagery almost tells another tale, at least one beyond Edward's immediate comprehension, as it collects the ominous and the beautiful into the human tensions around the fears of both passion and loss:

> One morning soon after we arrived, the row of tall trees outside my window were covered with small pale flowers too fragile to resist the wind. They fell in a day, and looked like snow on the rough grass—snow with a faint sweet scent. Then they were blown away.
>
> The fine weather lasted longer. It lasted all that week and the next and the next and the next. No sign of a break. My fever weakness left me, so did all misgiving.
>
> I went very early to the bathing pool and stayed there for hours, unwilling to leave the river, the trees shading it, the flowers that opened at night. They were tightly shut, drooping, sheltering from the sun under their thick leaves.
>
> It was a beautiful place—wild, untouched, above all untouched, with an alien, disturbing, secret loveliness. And it kept its secret. I'd find myself thinking, 'What I see is nothing—I want what it *hides*—that is not nothing.'(87)

For both Edward and Antoinette their honeymoon is a journey, metaphorical as well as real. Edward, smug that he has captured a beautiful if strange and exotic woman with a substantial dowry, feels little emotion and far less love for his bride—a condition not unusual among second sons in Victorian families who must get along on their own—but from the beginning he is aware that he must depend upon her, for this enclosed and intoxicating world where she is leading him is 'not only wild but menacing'.(69) The journey, of course, ends in failure for a number of reasons, not the least of which is Edward's inability to accept any dependence which gradually becomes apparent. His motives for marrying Antoinette, callous from the beginning, are not, however, the source of the failure of the marriage; it is finally his inability and refusal to give of himself. His sense of responsibility for her proceeds from his code of honour, not from love. Antoinette's own disengagement, her enclosed world, contribute to the impossibility of their marriage. She desires closeness, but closeness circumscribed by her own narrow universe, which is strange and threatening to Edward.

For Antoinette their trip is not only a return but an escape—a chance to recapture some lost tranquility of childhood and avoid, for a short time at least, the responsibilities and further displacement of her marriage. The complex of emotions which compel Antoinette to return to her past elude Edward completely from the beginning. He does, however, begin to realise how fundamentally disparate he and his wife are, and the significance of his realisation becomes increasingly apparent to him.

As he is led deeper into the natural landscape, however, he is forced to see Antoinette as more than a testament to his enterprise. He sees her as a human being, and in so doing he partially sees for the first time the wide cultural and emotional gulf which separates them. Recognition brings deeper doubts and fear:

> She never blinks at all it seems to me. Long, sad, dark alien eyes. Creole of pure English descent she may be, but they are not English or European either. And when did I begin to notice all this about my wife Antoinette? After we left Spanish Town I suppose. Or did I notice it before and refuse to admit what I saw? Not that I had much time to notice anything. I was married a month after I arrived in Jamaica and for nearly three weeks of that time I was in bed with fever.(67)

That all of these reactions are new to him, and that he is unable to assimilate them, is indicated by the wide range of mood and feeling that he exhibits during the short trip to the cottage. And as he begins to know more of his wife and she appears increasingly alien and strange to him, he gradually begins to identify her with the blacks, as the lines above imply.

For both of them, however, it is this lush, mysterious jungle that works on them, in opposite ways, and lays bare their passions and fears. For Edward, 'everything is too much', and this feeling extends to the entire natural scene: 'Too much blue, too much purple, too much green. The flowers too red, the mountains too high, the hills too near.'(70) Yet his instincts are also awakened by these same surroundings and the startlingly attractive girl he has married; he is ambivalent; Antoinette is 'beautiful. And yet. . . .'(70, ellipsis in text). The primitive beauty of the country has about it a pristine quality, 'an intoxicating freshness as if all this had never been breathed before'. (73) For Edward it had not, and this is part of its seductive quality.

The whole exotic experience of the first few days at Granbois is a kind of initiation for Edward. There is a dominant sensual element to nearly everything, and it is as though he were entering upon some erotic rite where every scene and act has a meaning beyond itself. Like all initiates to an alien experience, 'the feeling of security had left him'.

It is important to observe carefully Edward's initial emotions, because they explain if not condone his later behaviour toward Antoinette. From the beginning he finds himself in a world at once seductive and hostile, so far distant from his English roots that there is little in his past which has prepared him to understand much of what he observes: 'As for my confused impressions they will never be written. There are blanks in my mind that cannot be filled up.'(76) His confusion only increases as the days in this remote place with Antoinette pass.

His reactions of puzzlement and mistrust slowly begin to transfer themselves to Antoinette, and his changing perceptions of her only deepen his apprehensions. At one point she asks him if he thinks, '"that I have slept too long in the moonlight?"'.(83) For Edward there is about Atoinette a kind of lunar association, and for him the moon becomes a kind of 'objective correlative' of Antoinette. It is an association through which his insecurity and suspicions are apparent. Like Rhys's heroines before her, Antoinette senses some fatal flaw within herself, some curious turn of mind that will eventually collapse the will, a sense at once as indefinite and ominous as Edward's association of her with the moon.

It is more with a false bravado, I believe, than with a treacherous will that Edward recounts the first of their passionate unions:

There was no one in the house and only two candles in the room which had been so brilliantly lit. Her room was dim, with a shaded candle by the bed and another on the dressing-table. There was a bottle of wine on the round table. It was very late when I poured out two glasses and told her to drink to our happiness, to our love and the day without end which would be tomorrow. I was young then. A short youth mine was.(84)

For a few short days and nights after this both of them are locked in an oblivion of sensual gluttony, the intensity of which obscures the borders of a darker meaning and fear. The passion itself is induced more by the lushness and sensuousness of their environment than by mutual response. Antoinette is drawn to Edward by a desperate urgency to bring him into her private world, to live naturally and passiontely within the rhythms of the natural environment she knows. But it is a world which Edward can neither accept nor understand. Edward recognises that this inordinate expression of passion without the deeper resonance of love, at least on his part, releases too much: 'It was not a safe game to play. Desire, Hatred, Life, Death come very close in the darkness.'(94) Also, these large emotions and questions that passion released needed to be confronted in union, and Edward and Antoinette remained in their mutual isolation. Furthermore, it is clear that this unstable idyll will break with the same intensity and passion that gave it shape; the atmosphere itself is as deep with foreboding as it is with sensuality. The desperate quality of Antoinette's passion and the callousness with which Edward accepts it is seemingly typical of the male—female relationship which Rhys created in her earlier work, except that in this case the female is more a participant than an object. This difference, however, does not diminish the desperate quality, it only heightens the sense of inevitable tragic outcome. The exclusive quality of Antoinette's desire for Edward represents a withdrawal from all other outward connections into isolation which is an escape into her own private world, and, as we have seen, isolation is the condition of despair for Rhys's heroines.

The letter Edward receives from the mulatto, Daniel Cosway, who claims to be Antoinette's half-brother, the son of her father by a black woman, is the first overt intrusion of the outside world. It tells Edward of the madness of Antoinette's mother. It can be argued that the appearance of the letter is the thread of evidence that Edward has been looking for—an excuse to put into effect a plan that will allow him to return to England and no longer have to act as a husband, but only as a caretaker to Antoinette. But such conniving is, it seems to me, beyond Edward's capability. He is a dogged Englishman whose thought and values have crystalised; he is the egocentric male figure so convinced of his 'higher level of feeling' and intelligence that he can see no other point of view. He is blind rather than deliberately malicious.

The psychological movement of the novel, however, is governed as much by what Edward does not explain as by what he does. Cosway's letter provides the dramatic turning point, and Edward's reaction to the revelation of its contents reveals his inauthentic feelings for Antoinette and his own false pride rather than the first intimations of some sinister plan that has lain hidden only to be set in motion by some external event. Rhys's characterisation has been far too subtle for such clarity of purpose to emerge suddenly from Edward. The tone of Edward's narrative suggests self-pity rather than self-justification and the dominant mood is one of sadness not revenge.

More than anything else, Cosway's letter releases the unexpressed and implied emotions which remained in abeyance during the first days at Granbois; the abridged feelings begin to emerge with rapid and horrible force. When Edward finally meets with Cosway, Cosway tells him of Antoinette's relationship with Sandi, a young black:

> She start with Sandi. They fool you well about that girl. She look you straight in the eye and talk sweet talk—and it's lies she tell you. Lies. Her mother was so. They say she worse than her mother, and she hardly more than a child. Must be you deaf you don't hear people laughing when you marry her.(125)

Edward's response to Cosway's revelation is self-righteous—even fearful. It reminds me somewhat of Gabriel Conroy's reaction to his wife's, Gretta's, recollection of her dead lover Michael Fury in Joyce's 'The Dead', not in the mode of revelation, but rather in the way in which the two men's egos operate. Lacking the generosity of spirit which would enable him to accept or at least understand this very human desire for contact and leap from loneliness, Edward is wounded and outraged. Like Gabriel, Edward's inflated pride and imperious personality entrap his feelings exclusively in the self. The implications of Edward's reactions also reveal not only a central moral question in the novel, but the deeply rooted conflict in the natures of both himself and Antoinette. Violating as it does what is for Edward a gigantic taboo, Antoinette's relationship with Sandi confirms the impossibility of union on Edward's part. Throughout the narrative Edward presents his values as the normative ones, and from this point on he sees Antoinette as forever savage and given to self-abandonment in lust. In failing to love her he also fails to comprehend her. Also, like Gabriel Conroy, locked in his own ego, he can at best feel pity, an emotion far less costly than love. And his pity justifies his sense of honour. His male hubris not only limits the quality of his responsibility, it enfeebles his reason.

The latent antagonisms of both Edward and Antoinette are set loose by Cosway's revelation and the actions which follow—desperate on the part of Antoinette and self-assertive yet confused on the part of Edward—bring the violent forces within the novel to their climax. The deeper racial prejudices, and the compelling but ominous environment begin to recede from prominence as Antoinette and Edward confront the mystery of each other and inevitably fail to understand the sources of their opposition. Two scenes, both explicitly sexual, reveal not only their widely opposed natures, but the deeper psychological forces which motivate them.

Antoinette, desperate to keep Edward, visits Christophine, the wise old native woman who practices obeah. Christophine's involvement in the novel from this point on becomes increasingly prominent. Her position is ambiguous, and yet she has the clearest head of all. Besides her suspected powers in the black arts, she sees clearly through Edward's motives and recognises the futility of Antoinette's desperate struggle to capture Edward's love. Christophine at first advises her to flee, but Antoinette explains to her the 'white laws' which subjugate her; nevertheless, Antoinette entertains the notion of escape, and in a moving passage imagines what England would be like for her.

I have been too unhappy, I thought, it cannot last, being so unhappy, it would kill you. I will be a different person when I live in England and different things will happen to me . . . . England, rosy pink in the geography book map, but on the page opposite the words are closely crowded, heavy looking. Exports, coal, iron, wool. Then Imports and Character of Inhabitants. Names, Essex, Chelmsford on the Chelmer. The Yorkshire and Lincolnshire wolds. Wolds? Does that mean hills? How high? Half the height of ours, or not even that? Cool green leaves in the short cool summer. There are fields of corn like sugar-cane fields, but gold colour and not so tall. After summer the trees are bare, then winter and snow. White feathers falling? Torn pieces of paper falling? They say frost makes flower patterns on the window panes. I must know more than I know already. For I know that house where I will be cold and not belonging, the bed I shall lie in has red curtains and I have slept there many times before, long ago. How long ago? In that bed I will dream the end of my dream. But my dream had nothing to do with England and I must not think like this, I must remember about chandeliers and dancing, about swans and roses and snow. And snow.(111)

Her image of England is gradually dominated by cold and snow, all of its features set in careful contrast to the warmth of her native land. England holds no hope for her; it is cold, menacing, isolated, dead.

Against Christophine's advice, Antoinette pleads with her to practice obeah in order to bring Edward back to her: '"But Christophine, if he, my husband, could come to me one night. Once more. I would make him love me."'(113) Christophine knows that the primitive gods of the Islands are, in the end, helpless against the coldness of the Englishman, but she is moved to help Antoinette. Antoinette, of course, longs to return to what she imagined to be that idyllic state during those early days after she and Edward's arrival at Granbois. In spite of the violence in her life, she is still innocent, unable to accept the fact that their union was for Edward a business transaction, and he is incapable of accepting anything more, and certainly not love, which was never a part of the deal he made with her step-brother. And, ironically enough, those very qualities in Antoinette which attract him are the ones which he fears the most: the fundamental flaw in Antoinette's plan lies in her assumption that sexual passion can evoke and redeem love. It is a terrible irony that leaves the couple at cross-purposes. There is no unifying element where the two of them can meet; there is no context to join them. Edward can never allow himself to lose control, to abandon the self, and for Antoinette to attempt to bring them together through obeah will leave him to despise her forever.

While Antoinette visits Christophine, Edward and the villainous Daniel Cosway finally meet. This scene is carefully placed in ironic juxtaposition with the previous one. Here we have another older figure of the Islands giving advice to the young. The obvious clue to his reliability as opposed to Christophine's is that in the end he demands £500 silence money from Edward, whereas Christophine insists that Antoinette pay her nothing. Cosway not only reiterates to Edward the story of Antoinette's mother's madness, but tells him of Antoinette's relationship with the black boy, Sandi, with no intention of doing either Antoinette or Edward any good. The revelation enrages Edward, but by the time he confronts Antoinette his mood has changed.

'I do not hate you, I am most distressed about you, I am distraught,' I said. But this was untrue, I was not distraught, I was calm, it was the first time I had felt calm or self-possessed for many a long day.(127)

Antoinette tells him for the first time about her family and includes her account of her last visit to her mother: 'Then she seemed to grow tired and sat down in the rocking-chair. I saw the man lift her up out of the chair and kiss her. I saw his mouth fasten on hers and she went all soft and limp in his arms and he laughed.'(134)

The explicit sexual domination which Antoinette describes deepens his fears of Antoinette's own possible madness and strengthens his sense of the sinister powers which surround him. He, nevertheless, remains physically susceptible to his 'moon-drenched' wife; she is momentarily transformed by his own sexual desires into an erotic temptress:

The light changed her. I had never seen her look so gay or so beautiful. She poured wine into two glasses and handed me one but I swear it was before I drank that I longed to bury my face in her hair as I used to do. I said, 'We are letting ghosts trouble us.' (136-37)

But his aroused sexual feelings will give him all the more reason to feel repelled by her later. Antoinette has placed the drug which Christophine gave her in Edward's wine glass and he drinks it. Although the ensuing scene is withheld from the narrative by Rhys, Edward recalls upon awakening that 'I will always swear that she need not have done it.'(137) This is psychologically untrue, for to give in to the passions which Antoinette released in him represented a union which was intolerable, because he could not dominate, control, or completely exercise his will, and for Edward such a union would

be antithetical to his nature. This is the real source of his fear—his own
violent passions which Antoinette released and which he saw as
leaving him exposed and vulnerable to another person. In other
words, he fears the closeness of relationship—he fears love. Obeah's
powers can raise the passions in man, but they cannot create love
where it does not exist. Edward is essentially a figure who despises
passion and because the seductive beauty of the island and
Christophine's drug temporarily filled him with passion, he will
despise Antoinette as something alien and hostile to him, but his
pathetic sense of honour will endure.

The next morning, when the effects of the drug wear off, he recalls
dreaming that he had been 'buried alive'. He is confused; he looks
around the room and focuses on the objects surrounding the orgy of
the night before. His thoughts are those of '. . . a child spelling out
the letters of a word which he cannot read, and which if he could,
have no meaning or context'.(137) He is disoriented as he tries to
remember his abandonment. Finally he fixes his gaze on the sleeping,
spent figure of Antoinette, who is still a sensual and erotic figure, but
seeing her as the source of his having been brought over the edge
of passion and control, hate wells up in him. His entire being
rebles.

It is still in this state that he takes the black servant girl Amelie to
bed, just 'behind the thin partition which divided us from my wife's
bedroom'.(140) It is a deliberate act of revenge—an act which
dramatises his hostility and need to dominate, which symbolises his
essential attitude toward life. He affronts Antoinette and, equally
important, the marriage itself. When it is over he feels no remorse; he
is 'satisfied and peaceful'. He has demonstrated to himself the power
of his maleness—an ego far stronger than little Antoinette or her gods
can oppose—but in so doing he has shown us his ability to destroy
Antoinette. The powers of love which Antoinette called upon have
been transformed by Edward's ego into hatred.

Near the close of Part II Christophine points out to Edward his real
sin, 'nobody is to have any pride but you'.(150) He is not in the end a
scoundrel intent upon destroying Antoinette; rather he wants a
relationship which guarantees both his protection and Antoinette's.
We feel by the end of the novel that he would have been quite willing
to assume a marriage at a distance, but Antoinette's passionate and
naïve being would never accept this. Edward comes from another
world and cannot fathom the life of the passions; everything in the
natural surroundings which epitomises sensuous beauty tells him that

this is Antoinette's world, and this is why he fears it from the beginning.

Christophine, with her uncanny wisdom, understands Edward. She says to him, ' "to me you are not the best, nor the worst" '.(156) Christophine is right in the end, but this observation deepens rather than lessens our sense of Antoinette's misery. Antoinette retreats into herself and inevitably goes mad. And Edward—his pathos is hatred, an emotion which links him more strongly to Antoinette than love ever could.

Part III of the novel is a code which confirms Antoinette's wretched destiny. The novel's denouement occurs at the end of Part II as Edward and Antoinette leave Granbois on horseback and we recall her exuberance, happiness, and promise as she leads Edward up to the mountain retreat. The full tragedy lies in the fact that Edward could see a glimmer of that promise but could not realise it, and in his misplaced hatred: 'Above all I hated her. For she belonged to the magic and the loveliness. She had left me thirsty and all my life would be thirst and longing for what I had lost before I found it.'(172) Edward could not find it amid all the loveliness and magic because he could not allow himself to look, and Antoinette, who offered it, could not understand his fear.

But there is something uneasy and vaguely unsatisfying about these closing implications as well as in the entire thematic movement of *Wide Sargasso Sea*. In spite of its insights into the male–female relationship, it is a disturbing text, because underneath the brilliant surface qualities and revealing delineation of character, there is a lingering doubt that the dominant emotion, always subtly rendered, is somehow wide of the mark. At the heart of this reservation is the characterisation of Antoinette. Somewhere Elizabeth Bowen writes that it is not our fate but our business to lose innocence, and once we have lost it it is futile to attempt a picnic in Eden. However much blame the reader places upon Edward for Antoinette's tragic demise—admittedly my own reading of the novel does not view Edward as malicious in spite of his cold self-interest—there is something hollow in Antoinette's character which is covered over by the exotic and mysterious qualities Rhys gives to her. The nature of her passion and the sincerity of her feeling are not enough to establish that quality of empathy which attention to the themes of the novel demands.

The heroines in Rhy's four earlier novels, in spite of their frequent lassitude and indirection, have in varying degrees not only an instinct for survival but an understanding of human nature and the world that is completely lacking in Antoinette. This does not make the earlier heroines appear less vulnerable, but it does make them more fully realised characters. For example, the young Anna Morgan in *Voyage in the Dark*, for all of her naïveté, is engaged in both the world outside and the private world of the self; whereas Antoinette never gropes beyond the world of her childhood, and this fact alone reduces the quality of her relationship from the beginning. It is in the limitations in the characterisation of Antoinette, it seems to me, that the demands Rhys imposed upon her novel by using *Jane Eyre* reveal themselves as too confining. On the whole, her autobiographical background enriches the entire fabric of *Wide Sargasso Sea*, but in the end, in revealing brilliantly the internal source of Antoinette's ultimate pathological condition, she must diminish the full impact of the tragedy of Antoinette's and Edward's marriage. The conclusion of the novel implies a lost meeting ground for love, where there was never one to be found. My point is not that this subtle conflict violates the informing principle of the novel, but rather that the reader is left with a conceptual problem in his final judgment of Edward. If it were simply a question of his taking advantage of a young innocent, there would be no problem, but the denouement of the novel implies in its description of Edward's loss that somehow he and Antoinette could have formed a vital union had only he been more open and generous. But if I understand Antoinette, a mature union would have been impossible because of her own limited capacity for understanding. Perhaps the argument of the novel is embodied in this very subtlety with which I have trouble, but it seems that Antoinette's innocence is not only the major source of her own failure, it also reduces the quality of her entire relationship with Edward and in so doing lessens our sense of his incapacity to love which the novel, conversely, implies.

Wide Sargasso Sea, even with its exotic setting, its links with *Jane Eyre*, its more explicit qualities of narration, is not all that far distant from Rhys's novels of the 1930s. If not a fulfillment, it is certainly an extension of her most basic themes, and the same quality of feeling pervades *Wide Sargasso Sea* as the earlier novels. In spite of the limitations which I see in the characterisation of Antoinette, the novel's achievement is considerable, especially in the way it captures with a lyrical intensity the rhythm between the physical and metaphysical world. Furthermore, the novel's importance to Rhys's career is tremendous. In order to understand this it is necessary to view *Wide Sargasso Sea* in a wider context.

More than twenty-five years passed before Jean Rhys followed *Good Morning, Midnight* with another novel. As I pointed out in the first chapter, these mute years—marked by long period of with- drawal from any attempt to write—were not an admission that her powers were spent, as the publication of *Wide Sargasso Sea* finally confirmed. Francis Wyndham in his introduction, published in the first and all subsequent editions, suggests a literary and historical context to explain, partially at least, Rhys's long absence.

> After *Good Morning, Midnight*, Jean Rhys disappeared and her five books went out of print. Although these had enjoyed a critical success, their true quality had never been appreciated. The reason for this is simple: they were ahead of their age, both in spirit and in style. One has only to compare Miss Rhys's early books, written during the 1920s, with contemporary work by Katherine Mans- field, Aldous Huxley, Jean Cocteau, and other celebrated writers of the period, to be struck by how little the actual text has 'dated': the style belongs to today. More important, the novels of the 1930s are much closer in *feeling* [italics in text] to life as it is lived and understood in the 1960s than to the accepted attitudes of their time. The elegant surface and the paranoid content, the brutal honesty of the feminine psychology and the muted nostalgia for lost beauty, all create an effect which is peculiarly modern.[9]

It is impossible to measure with any precision these personal and external factors, but Wyndham's observations are, I believe, acute. His explanation accounts in part for the startling success of *Wide Sargasso Sea*, and implicit in it is the suggestion that Rhys herself had a clear sense through the 1940s and 1950s that in retrospect her work had achieved only limited success because the dominant sensibility contained in it was not sympathetically understood by the con- temporary reading public. While not content with a *success d'estime* for her work, she had at least achieved that, but little in the way of an audience.

It is all too easy now to accept the Rhys success story as solidified by the popular press and sealed as it were by A. Alvarez's assertion in the *New York Times*, frequently quoted on the American paperback editions, that Rhys is 'the best living English novelist'. In a more recent edition this claim has been shortened to simply 'the best living novelist'. Unlike most claims to literary discovery, this one, made chiefly on the merits of *Wide Sargasso Sea*, contains a strong element of truth, but it is not altogether accurate. At least two significant things occurred during those long years between the publication of *Good Morning, Midnight* and *Wide Sargasso Sea*. In May of 1957 Selma Vaz Dias performed her dramatic adaptation of *Good Morning, Midnight* on the BBC's Third Programme, and also wrote an article about Rhys in the *Radio Times* (3 May 1957). Equally important, Francis Wyndham himself wrote a brief but sensitive appreciation in *The London Magazine* several years later (January, 1960). The same issue also included Rhys's important short story, 'Till September Petronella'. These earlier appreciations, far from destroying the remarkable impact of *Wide Sargasso Sea* on the literary world and on Rhys's career, confirm it and provide a context. Francis Wyndham's role was significant, for it was he who spoke enthusiastically of Rhys's work to Diana Athill at Andre Deutsch, who bought an option on the novel in 1957 and agreed to follow its publication by republishing two of her earlier novels. So, in a sense, Rhys was rediscovered nearly ten years before the publication of *Wide Sargasso Sea*. It remained, however, for the critics and readers to respond so overwhelmingly to the novel itself, and this they clearly did. And the recognition and acclaim accorded *Wide Sargasso Sea* has brought both serious and popular if belated attention to the novels of the thirties and established Rhys's significance as a writer.

The effects of Rhys's expansion of character, subject matter and treatment of the material from *Jane Eyre* present interesting challenges for the reader of both texts. Critical studies of *Wide Sargasso Sea* have accounted for the way in which Rhys incorporated the basic elements and themes of the Brontë novel and used her own knowledge of the West Indies with skill to amplify and in effect, create new characterisations. In short, the way in which Rhys used *Jane Eyre* as the basis for her novel is fairly clear to us, but there are two other observations which need to be made. The first is fairly obvious; most novels which emerge from other novels are usually sequels—treatments of the fictional world after the conclusion of the first work. Sequels allow for much more latitude but are invariably inferior, imitative, and sterile. Rhys undertook a much more demanding task; the outcome of the plot, the direction of the narration, the fate of the characters, all, in a way were formed. But this predetermined outcome offered a number of advantages of which Rhys was clearly aware: although what lay at the end of the road was settled, it permitted her to concentrate on the road itself—the tale of the telling rather than the telling of the tale—an emphasis which had always been in her work from the beginning.

The reader's built-in curiosity about the shadowy Bertha from *Jane Eyre*, preserves plot interest and allows Rhys to concentrate on those aspects of her novel which most concerned her anyway—the cultural, racial and psychological forces which played on Antoinette, and, more importantly, the devastating effects she and Edward had on each other, for, as I have tried to indicate, their relationship lies at the heart of *Wide Sargasso Sea*, even though many other aspects of the novel challenge our interest. In fact, the limitations imposed by developing her novel out of *Jane Eyre* and the way in which Rhys dealt with them, even with the difficulty of Antoinette, in the development, design, and narrative control of her own novel became the sources of her considerable achievement.

A second point to be considered is the effect of this relationship on the reader. Readers have quite naturally accounted for the way in which Rhys incorporated the Brontë material and how the reader's knowledge of *Jane Eyre* is fundamental to an appreciation of *Wide Sargasso Sea*; but equally important, I believe, is the way in which the latter novel enriches and even transforms our understanding of the former. To re-read *Jane Eyre* after reading *Wide Sargasso Sea* is a startling experience. It is a feeling different from that which Eliot discusses in his essay 'Tradition and the Individual Talent' when he speaks of the way literature transforms our understanding of previous literature, or of the way in which reading Joyce's *Ulysses* enriches our experience and understanding of the *Odyssey*. *Wide Sargasso Sea* focuses the reader both within and before the spatio-temporal frame of *Jane Eyre*; it amplifies our considerations of character formation within *Jane Eyre* and even tests our sense of enclosure of a narrative text. Obviously this point raises a number of theoretical issues that are far too broad for our consideration here. My point, however, is that there is a more complex process going on for the reader of *Wide Sargasso Sea* involving more than simple recognition of the use of *Jane Eyre* in Rhys's text. The text of *Jane Eyre* is expanded by the reader's participation in *Wide Sargasso Sea*, and the aesthetic awareness is widened. Surely when we re-read *Jane Eyre* after reading *Wide Sargasso Sea* our participation in that experience is transformed; our considerations of Rochester and certainly of Bertha are more deeply engaged.

Although *Jane Eyre* ends in matrimonial fulfillment, an achievement of balance between the elements of nature and personality, and a discovery of mature love, a recognition of an essential unity among all of these potentially warring elements, the affirming emphasis of the novel is on human passion. *Wide Sargasso Sea* poses the same affirmation of passion but without the measures of control achieved through reconciliation of these elements in the natural order which externalise our internal conflicts. Rhys's novel is a study in unfulfillment, in unreconciled oppositions and contrasts—between cultures, races, temperaments, the sexes, and, above all, the way in which human beings perceive the world, each other and themselves in such widely opposing ways. The novel is not a one-sided treatment of any of these oppositions; on the contrary, it achieves its unity and renders its theme by a thorough recognition and exploration of all of them. And therein lies the great source of its final achievement.

7 The Later Writing

Wide Sargasso Sea was both a critical and popular success and its publication had spectacular and far-reaching, if belated, effects on Rhys's literary career. For the first time—after over forty years—her work came to the attention of a substantial number of readers. On the basis of their success with *Wide Sargasso Sea*, her publisher brought back into print virtually all of her earlier work, and the steady sales encouraged Penguin to publish her work in paperback. By the early seventies all of her work was available in both hardcover and paperback. Her critical reputation from the middle sixties through the seventies has grown steadily. Critics have pointed primarily to her strong originality and her remarkable insight into the feminine psyche, and, lying beneath most of the praise, is the collective recognition that Rhys simply writes like nobody else; her talent and intelligence encompass dimensions not found elsewhere in the modern English novel. The increasing interest in her work is to some extent a result of the growing attention that has been paid to women artists and of the recognition of women generally, but this development accounts only in part for her reputation. It is not only because readers are more attuned to the feminine consciousness that Rhys has gained such wide attention, but, more significantly, it has come to be recognised that her work explores with compassion and a rare intelligence the panic and emptiness of modern life and it does this within the consciousness of the female.

Since the publication of *Wide Sargasso Sea*, Rhys has thus far published three books. The first, *Tigers Are Better-Looking*, appeared in 1968. A volume of short fiction, it includes nine stories from *The Left Bank*, a segment from Ford's original introduction, and eight additional stories, all of which had appeared in various periodicals throughout the 1960s. *Sleep It Off, Lady* (1976), a second collection of short stories, brings together a group of mostly unpublished stories, but many of them predate, at least in initial composition, the eight new stories in *Tigers Are Better-Looking*. A third volume, *My Day* (1975), is a privately printed gathering of three 'pieces', autobio-

graphical sketches really. Given the careful composition and seemingly
endless rewriting that Rhys does before reaching a final draft, these
three volumes represent a substantial amount of work, especially
when we consider the author's great age and delicate health. This later
work does not exceed her earlier achievement, but, in fact, seems to
parallel it on a smaller scale except for the last stories in *Sleep It Off,
Lady*, with no slackness or diminution of her original powers. The
later stories are characterised by those same qualities of subtle
brilliance, acute observation, clarity of focus (in most of them), and
that remarkable balance and sense of proportion which all of her
mature work possesses. Furthermore, the new stories from *Tigers Are
Better-Looking* and *Sleep It Off, Lady* represent her full development as
a short-story writer. More ample in theme and range of sympathy,
they also reveal a versatility and technical mastery of the genre that
was only initiated in *The Left Bank*.

The first, longest, and one of the best stories in *Tigers Are Better-
Looking*, 'Till September Petronella', deals with a young model,
Petronella Gray, who lives in a bleak Bloomsbury bed-sitter and
plans to spend a fortnight in the country with Marston, a young
painter. Also staying in the cottage are his friend, Julian, a music critic,
and Julian's current lover, Frankie. After one night there Petronella,
no longer able to withstand the tensions in the house and Julian's
verbal assaults, returns to London. The story is remarkable for its
depiction of the surface and underlying tensions at this neurotic
gathering. From the beginning the theme is clearly revealed and
relentlessly pursued. The group at the cottage and the events
described portray a war—as old and as brutal as any other—between
the sexes. This story is closely related in theme to an uncollected story
of Rhys's which appeared in *Penguin Modern Stories 1* (1969), 'I Spy a
Stranger', which also demonstrates the polarisation of the sexes, in a
condition where men and women are natural adversaries.[1] Images of
the battlefield abound in 'I Spy a Stranger' and reflect the war that
goes on between the sexes.

Although much younger, Petronella reminds us of Laura in 'I Spy a
Stranger' in that she is like those women who draw male animosity
simply by their presence, and in Petronella's case it seems she is unable
to defend herself against men. As Petronella unpacks her things when
she first arrives Frankie discusses with her the biological inferiority of
women, and from there radiate the lines drawn in this war of social
and sexual relationships between men and women. And even after

Petronella exits through a window, events confirm that there is really no escape from the battle.

The title itself confirms and adds further ironic dimensions to the story's theme. Dates seldom appear in Rhys's work especially as they relate to historical events, but here a date confers important meaning to the story itself. After having stolen away from the cottage, Petronella is driven into town by a farmer, and while she waits for him to carry on some business in town before taking her to pick up her things at the cottage and putting her on a train to London, she sits in a pub eating tea and cakes. As she looks around the 'small, dark, stuffy room', her eyes come upon two calendars: 'One said January 9th, but the other was right—July 28th, 1914 . . . .' (ellipses in text)[2] In only a few short weeks the war of guns and trenches would begin, and for the reader the desperate quality of life that Petronella lives is made all the more ominous, and a trim and more catastrophic ironic meaning is given by the title. September, when her 'friends' return from the country, far from bringing any relief, will only confirm the underlying human barbarism on a grander and more violent scale.

Of Rhys's earlier heroines Petronella is closest to Anna Morgan of *Voyage in the Dark*. She seems to be an extension of the Anna whom the doctor at the end of the novel following the abortion confidently predicted would be 'ready to start all over again in no time'. The careful composition of place at the beginning of the story, with its description of Petronella's Bloomsbury surroundings as she is preparing to leave for the country, characteristically frames the attitude of the heroine as it describes her world. The landscape itself pulses with feeling as Petronella prepares to quit this confining life for a brief period. She had, as so frequently happens to Rhys's heroines, 'struck a bad patch', and 'she hated those streets, which were like a gray nightmare in the sun'.(11–12) Instead of being an escape from the bleak Bloomsbury world, Petronella's brief visit to the country brings out more clearly than ever to her the hopelessness of her situation, but, at the same time, the experience confirms for her the need to defend one's self against the enemy. Viewed on one level, the story can be seen as an indictment of easy masculine chauvinism and sexist attitudes which dominate most male–female relationships: as Petronella's experience reveals, a woman cannot afford innocence in this world, but neither is its loss a guarantee of survival if male aggression is indiscriminate. But at its deeper reaches the story explores the underside of behaviour and feeling as human beings knowingly and unknowingly torment each other, and the ultimate helplessness of women against male aggression.

Petronella is the Rhys feminine type that we have seen throughout her novels: intuitive, capable of bitter humour toward herself and those around her, trapped in a depressing environment, dependent upon and vulnerable to men and yet somehow steeled against what she knows will be eventual abuses. Petronella has not yet progressed very far along that inevitable downward spiral of life already travelled by Rhys's older heroines, who are wise in their knowledge of men but at the same time long for love; Petronella is young enough to build some defenses, but by the end of the story she is aware that ultimately they too will fail.

The four male characters in the story have been outlined for us in previous novels; they too embody in various ways (on a smaller scale, of course) the dominant male types and display the male attitudes toward women found in Rhys's novels. The weak Marston longs for a passionate relationship and yet fears it. He is not overtly cruel, but pathetic in his weakness that allows others to endure pain while he retreats into his private neurotic world. Marston allows Julian to attack and ridicule Petronella because males stand together against women no matter how antipathetic they are to each other. In Rhys's work it seems the stronger the male personality, the greater the capacity for human cruelty. The arrogant and hollow Julian draws strength from engaging in ridicule and cynicism. His tormented personality obviously seeks release through his mean verbal on-slaughts at Frankie and Petronella. He is an example of the bullying male who, having exploited women, through guilt or perversity has a sadistic desire to show them up as insincere and even villainous. Such an image of the female is necessary to justify his own uses of them. Petronella sees clearly his malignancy and spiritual emptiness: his 'beautiful eyes were little mean pits and you looked down into them into nothingness'.(24) The confident farmer who picks Petronella up along the road after she has escaped the cottage, and later takes her back to get her things and eventually puts her on the train for London, expresses more directly his attitude toward women. He sees his pleasures satisfied by what he believes is a fair and open exchange. With easy assurance he draws his stereotype of the male–female relationship, and the place women hold in his eyes: ' "They like a bit of loving, that's what they like, isn't it? A bit of loving. All women like that. They like it dressed up sometimes—and sometimes not, it all depends. You have to know, and I know. I just know." '(29) And with that talent for flat, cutting irony which we see so frequently in Rhys's heroines, Petronella replies: ' "You've nothing more to learn, have you?" '

The final male figure, Mr Melville, the young man whom she meets in a taxi upon arriving back at Paddington, is also a familiar Rhys type. Melville combines bravado with nervousness. Although not nearly so fully drawn, he reminds us, in his stops and starts with Petronella, of Horsfield in *Mr Mackenzie*. His advances, obvious but not without a leering charm, cause the bitter events at the cottage momentarily to recede from her thought. However, she recalls Marston's advice the night before: ' "Take my advice and grow another skin or two and sharpen your claws before it's too late. *Before it's too late*, [Italics in text] mark those words. If you don't, you're going to have a hell of a time." ' It is this advice and the nullifying effects of the entire visit, with its underlying tensions and Julian's ridicule and abuse, that prompt her to bare her 'claws'. She deals with Melville as directly as the combative Frankie dealt with Julian:

'We must see each other again.' he said. 'Please. Couldn't you write to me at—' He stopped. 'No, I'll write to you. If you're ever—I'll write to you anyway.'
. . . 'Do you know what I want? I want a gold bracelet with blue stones in it. Not too blue—the darker blue I prefer.'
'Oh, well.' He was wary again. 'I'll do my best, but I'm not one of these plutocrats, you know.'
'Don't you dare to come back without it. But I'm going away for a few weeks. I'll be here again in September.'(38)

But as she returns to her room she is aware that it is a Pyrrhic victory, only one slight victorious confrontation in a losing war.

The theme of survival always complements the theme of suffering and helplessness in Rhys's fiction, and 'Till September Petronella' is no exception. Rhys's considerable sympathy for her female victims of continued male exploitation not only diminishes what could be mere morbidity, but offers insight into and understanding of the ways women battle against impossible odds. It is in this shadow of hopelessness that Rhys discovers a vitality in her heroines, such as Petronella, that exposes essential truths of human nature. Her stories frequently complement and draw attention to the themes of her novels, but stories such as 'Till September Petronella' with its subtle

unity of tone and brilliant arrangement of detail remind us that
Rhys's achievement does not lie exclusively with the novel.

Most of the remaining new stories in this collection recall both in
setting and theme Rhys's earlier work. 'The Day They Burned the
Books', for example, is set in the West Indies. It is a story of adolescent
understanding and tenderness set against the caprice and ignorance of
the adult world. Rhys has treated this subject before in such stories as
'Again the Antilles', but in this story she exposes a vengeful ignorance
of which a child is the victim. 'Let Them Call It Jazz' returns to the
exile in its woeful portrait of a West Indian woman immigrant whose
only real possession is a melody she has composed in her head, which
is taken from her for five pounds. She is left thinking: 'I don't belong
nowhere really, and I haven't money to buy my way to belonging.'(67) 'Outside the Machine' is a curious and interesting story, for
it treats a subject that emerges frequently but is usually subdued in
Rhys's fiction: women's relationships with each other. And this story
ends on a note of kindness, of one woman toward another, that is
indeed rare in Rhys's world. 'A Solid House', set in London during
the blitz, also explores the tensions which emerge in the complex
relationships women have with each other.

The most dramatically intense of the new stories is the last, 'The
Sound of the River', a haunting and fearful account of a man and a
woman who have rented a remote cottage next to a river. The
woman, who narrates the story, is temporarily moved out of her
obsessional and premonition-laden private world by the horrible
reality of the man's death. After he had tried one night to comfort her
and quell her obsessive fears, he had appeared to drift off to sleep. But
when the narrator awakens to see the sun for the first time during their
stay, she realises that the man is dead, that he died the night before and
that she had lain next to him throughout the night. She comes to
realise, too, that reality itself is every bit as disturbing and menacing as
those fears locked inside of us. The river is analogous to the rhythm
and turmoil of life and its passing as it moves in its endless course.

The stories in *Sleep It Off, Lady* can be seen collectively to
form a kind of thematic coda, or retrospective chorus, to all of
Rhys's previous work. If the less successful ones leave the reader
with the feeling that this is material written long ago that for one
reason or another was discarded, the majority confirm the clarity of
focus that has always marked her work as well as that certainty of
feeling within that narrow world she draws upon for her subject
matter. The mood and view of the world that hovers over all of her

work is securely present in the stories in this volume. The progression of the sixteen stories, moving from youth and adolescence to adulthood and, inevitably, to old age, from Dominica to London, Paris and, finally, to Devon, are recognisable to the reader as an echo of Rhys's previous fiction. We can also see in these stories a retrospective progression that reveals a life as well as a substantial art. The last story, 'I Used to Live Here Once', gathers up many of the qualities and attitudes characteristic of Rhys's art in its richly symbolic depiction of the ultimate separation that occurs between not only youth and age but between all human beings because of their fears and conflicting needs. It charts the perilous journey one takes in life to arrive at that point of impotent wisdom and awful knowledge.

The last four stories in *Sleep It Off, Lady*, treating as they do the loneliness and frequent humiliation of old age, reveal in their depth of feeling and intensity Rhys's sustained powers of observation and sympathetic understanding of her characters. Rhys's treatment of the dreadful circumstances of these aged victims reminds us in an uncanny way of the themes and outlook found in her stories of childhood disillusionment—as though the very old and very young share the same vulnerability and the world itself looks upon them with the same sense of exclusion, but they in turn see, precisely because they are outsiders, the whole enterprise of life with a clarity of vision that penetrates the vulnerable façade of hypocrisy and prejudice which society erects to protect itself. Actually it is in the vision of these outsiders and victims that we come closest to Rhys's own view of the world and to her central thematic concerns. The most fully realised stories in *Sleep It Off, Lady* are those which treat the lost innocence of youth as it becomes aware of the adult world and the aged as they attempt to cope in a world insensitive to them.

The first story in the volume, 'Pioneers, Oh, Pioneers', concerns the fate of Mr Ramage, a young Englishman who comes to Dominica to buy an estate, as 'remote as possible'. He weds a coloured girl of dubious reputation and attempts to 'go native'. But to cross such a cultural gap is impossible. His behaviour is regarded as highly eccentric by both the natives and the white population. He is bitterly maligned by the whites and finally killed by the blacks. On the periphery of these events, but central to the story's theme, is the young girl Rosalie's identification with and sympathy for Ramage.

In the opening scene Rosalie and her young friend observe the absurd figure cut by an elderly Englishwoman who rides up the mountain in the heat in her heavy, dark riding habit and carries a huge chunk of ice, held by a blanket, that drips on her knee. In its absurdity and humour, this scene foreshadows the more important but equally ludicrous scene which seals Ramage's fate with the white community. Rosalie defends the old woman by saying, 'she wants her drinks cold', while her friend dismisses her as crazy. However, behaviour such as the old woman's is acceptable because it is merely identified as evidence of the legendary eccentricities within the English character.

But eccentricity on the part of the white man who identifies with the natives is labelled as barbaric by the majority of the whites and occasions less tolerant reaction. In a marvellously funny scene, Mr Eliot and his wife are out looking at some young nutmeg trees and have stopped to heat water for tea when they run into Ramage 'coming out from under the trees. He was burned a deep brown, his hair fell to his shoulders, his beard to his chest. He was wearing sandals and a leather belt, on one side of which hung a cutlass, on the other a large pouch. Nothing else.'[3] They are both shocked by the spectacle of this naked Englishman, but Mrs Eliot, with a degree of sophistication never seen before in the Islands says, '"Mr Ramage, the kettle is just boiling. Will you have some tea?"' But this little episode as recounted by Mr Eliot to the white settlement seals Ramage's fate, and he is hounded by both the natives and the whites until he is killed.

Rosalie sympathises strongly with Ramage and reveals in her sympathy a union with him which predicts her own fate. Her sensitivity will make her as vulnerable to the world as Ramage's eccentricities have made him. She is one of those women about whom Rhys will write again and again, whose special qualities of feeling inevitably lead to suffering and torment. Rather than finding support for their feelings, women such as Rosalie are repeatedly victimised by men and shunned by other women.

The second story in the volume, 'Goodbye Marcus, Goodbye Rose', deepens the theme of the lost innocence of childhood and focuses more emphatically on the intrusion of the adult world and its dramatic and far-reaching effects. The young girl in the story, Phoebe, is left at the conclusion of the tale with her entire outlook on life shaken, but her experience has become for her an awakening, a kind of rite of passage into adulthood:

> Well there was one thing. Now she felt very wise, very grown-up, she could forget these childish worries. She could hardly believe that only a few weeks ago she, like all the others, had

secretly made lists of her trousseau, decided on the names of her three children. Jack. Marcus. And Rose.

Now goodbye Marcus. Goodbye Rose. The prospect before her might be difficult and uncertain but it was far more exiciting.(30)

Although something is destroyed, and 'some vague irreparable loss saddened her', there is something to be gained, 'the fun of being grown-up and important, of doing what you wanted instead of what you were told to do, would start'.(30)

This manifest change in Phoebe's life is brought about by her encounter and subsequent visits with an old sea captain who takes her on long walks and one day places his hand on her breast. He does not fondle her, nor does Phoebe feel any sexual pleasure, but the psychological effect upon her is profound. She feels violated, seduced, but gradually she begins to feel as well that she has been initiated into another realm of experience, and somehow set apart from her friends, and, because it is also secret, separated from her family and drawn into a strange union with the randy old captain. Phoebe sees more of Captain Cardew, and during their long walks together he delights in telling her of love and passion; Phoebe is drawn to an identification with him that is no less intense because she senses something wicked in him and thus in herself. What we see in both of these stories is not only the way the intrusion of the adult world erases the protective cover of childhood from the young heroines, but, more importantly, the way in which these experiences, indirect in the first story, reveal to Rosalie and Phoebe particular sympathies within themselves to values and sensibilities which are opposed to those of the social world in which they were brought up. Rhys's account of these early experiences, although published much later, seem to prefigure the more developed and ultimately more self-destructive female sensibilities that we see in the heroines of her novels. Without making too much of these short works, the reader, nevertheless, gets the feeling that they are brief explorations into the early formation of a particular female consciousness that gradually sets itself apart from the established values and behaviour expected of women. These are young women who will choose ultimately to accept the consequences in a quest for freedom. And they somehow know full well from the beginning the nature of their risk, but because they do not know men they really have no sense of how perilous their journey will become.

While the early stories in *Sleep It Off, Lady* take us backward in a

way, the last four stories extend the range of Rhys's own sympathies
as she treats with considerable feeling and power the inevitable
humiliation and loneliness that comes to the elderly near the end of
their lives. These stories are remarkable for their intensity and depth
of feeling; they also possess a closeness to the experience in style and
utterance that the other stories in the volume, for all their polish, seem
to lack. As the characters in subsequent stories grow older and
approach death the narrative voice seems to reside more deeply in the
experiences as they unfold and become increasingly horrible. In
'Rapunzel, Rapunzel' the narrator, who is herself elderly, lies next to
an old woman, Mrs Peterson, in a convalescent home and watches
admiringly as she brushes her hair. She realises that, 'she must have
taken great care of it all her life and now there it all was, intact, to
comfort and reassure her that she was still herself'.(140–1) A few
days later a barber comes in and Mrs Peterson requests a trim and a
shampoo. The barber with 'a large pair of scissors' nearly cuts all of
her beautiful hair to the roots, and tells her, 'You'll be glad to be rid of
the weight of it, won't you dear?'(143) With a few clips of the scissors
Mrs Peterson is robbed, not of her vanity, but of the last comfort and
ressurance she had left, and shortly thereafter she dies. Told from the
point of view of the narrator-observer, who can identify with the old
woman, the story's brutally sad ending achieves enormous meaning.
Rhys's irony is brilliantly effective because it is dependent on the
narrator's cold recognition of the callousness with which Mrs
Peterson is stripped of her last symbol of self-respect. And the
narrator's own protective devices are revealed in the closing lines of
the story, which make us all the more aware of the narrator's own
struggle for life—a struggle all the more intense because of the
nearness of death and rejection by the living. Rejection in one form or
another lies deeply within these stories of old age. The title story,
'Sleep It Off, Lady', the most dramatically intense of the stories, traces
the fears and obsessions of the elderly to a horrible conclusion. And
the last story, 'I Used to Live Here Once', mentioned earlier, offers a
concluding vision of the inevitable separation between those who, to
use the story's own symbolism, have crossed the stream and those
who have not. A terrifying vision really, but the power of Rhys's art
has always resided in her ability to see most clearly those things within
us that separate and drive us apart.

The range of her subject matter has never been wide, but her
understanding of what it is to have been a woman in this century is
comprehensive. Written in a style that brings form and content into a

harmonious whole rarely equaled in modern fiction, her work reveals in its humour, sympathy, and understanding a fully realised and significant portrait of the female consciousness in the modern world.

Postscript

Jean Rhys died on the afternoon of 14 May, 1979. She was in the Royal Devon and Exeter Hospital, not far from her cottage in the village of Cheriton Fitzpaine where she had spent the last years of her life. A small, private ceremony for relatives and close friends was held in Exeter a week later. The obituaries recounted the familiar story of her career, the long years of obscurity, the belated recognition in her old age, and the growing stature of her literary reputation during the last dozen years. Her life had come to embrace, and in an extreme way typify, the plight and struggle of many women in this century for recognition and fulfillment. Her work, especially as it came to be seen through the sensibility of the seventies, also revealed in its themes and treatment vital truths of the condition of women in the modern world. Even her eventual success underscored the biting irony found in her work, for it came so terribly late in her long life, after seemingly endless years of pain and failure.

In one of the obituary notices Jean Rhys's friend and editor, Diana Athill, told a reporter that 'even when being taken to hospital last winter, she said to the nurse as the ambulance fetched her, "Please— my eye shadow."' Like a character in one of her own novels, she perhaps knew that women's small vanities are sometimes their only defence.

Notes

Preface

1. References to the more interesting profiles appear in the bibliography.

Chapter 1.

1. Biographical information in this chapter comes from a number of sources, nearly all of it through interviews. Very little substantial biographical information has been published on Jean Rhys. There have been a number of feature articles and interviews in the popular publications, and the more important ones are listed in the bibliography.

   I have interviewed or obtained information from the following: Jean Rhys, Robin Waterfield, Oliver Stoner, Charles Cox, William Tilden-Smith, Anne Smyser, Henriette van Eyk, Gerry Franken, John Byrne, and Diana Athill.

   The Jean Rhys Collection at The University of Tulsa is an essential resource for anyone studying the life and work of the author. Besides rich manuscript holdings and autobiographical material, there is a large collection of letters. A catalogue and description of this collection is currently being prepared.
2. Marcelle Bernstein, 'The Inscrutable Miss Rhys', *Observer Colour Magazine*, 1 June 1969.
3. There is some confusion about the material which Rhys gave Mrs Adam. In an interview she insists that it was not what was to become *The Left Bank* stories. Elgin Mellown in his essay (see bibliography), suggests that the stories were later published under *The Left Bank* title. Some of them may have been radically changed later and included in the volume, but several of the stories, because of their subject matter, were written after Rhys met Ford, and therefore, could not have been given to Mrs Adam. In any event, the stories or sketches, at least in the form given to Mrs Adam, have not survived.
4. Direct quote from an interview with Jean Rhys, Cheriton Fitzpaine, Devon, 7 June 1977.
5. Interview, 7 June 1977.
6. Stella Bowen, *Drawn From Life* (London, 1941), pp. 166–67.
7. Ford's affair with Gertrud is cited from Arthur Mizener's biography of Ford: *The Saddest Story*, (New York and Cleveland: World Publishing Company, 1971), p. 175. Mizener's account is taken in part from Violet Hunt's *The Flurried Years*. For further citations and information see endnote 10, p. 553, Mizener.
8. Edouard de Nève, *Barred* (London: Desmond Harmsworth, 1932), pp. 86–87.
9. de Nève, p. 128.

10. *Time*, 6 February 1978, p. 53.
11. Letter from Leslie Tilden-Smith to Anne Smyser, Hampstead, Dominica, 25 May 1936 (The University of Tulsa Collection).
12. Interview, Cheriton Fitzpaine, Devon, 11 August 1977.
13. Interview, 11 August 1977.
14. The correspondence with all of Jean Rhys's letters to Vaz Dias is in The University of Tulsa Rhys Collection.

Chapter 2

1. Jean Rhys, *The Left Bank* (London: Jonathan Cape, 1927). All subsequent references will be to this edition and will be incorporated into the text. This is the only one of Rhys's earlier works which has not been reprinted in its entirety in England. A later volume of stories, *Tigers Are Better-Looking* includes only a selection of stories from *The Left Bank*. The volume has been reprinted in the United States by Books for Libraries Press, Freeport, New York, 1970.
2. In his preface of over twenty pages, Ford spends only five on Rhys and her work; the rest is a rambling evocation of his own experiences and impressions of Paris.
3. George Wickes, *American In Paris 1903–1939*, (New York: Doubleday & Co. Inc. 1969), p. 3.
4. Ford Madox Ford, *The Good Soldier*, (New York: Vintage Books, n.d., but notice of copyright renewal, 1955), p. 4.
5. Ford Madox Ford, *The Good Soldier*, p. 5.
6. Mark Schorer, 'An Interpretation', in *The Good Soldier*, p. vi.
7. Germaine Bree, *Women Writers in France* (New Brunswick, New Jersey: Rutgers University Press, 1973) p. 7.
8. *TLS*, 5 May 1927, p. 320.
9. *The New York Times Book Review*, 10 February 1929, p. 8.
10. *Saturday Review of Literature*, 5 November 1927, p. 287.

Chapter 3

1. Jean Rhys, *Quartet* (London, 1969). Originally published by Chatto and Windus under the title, *Postures*, in 1928, but Simon and Schuster issued it in 1929 as *Quartet*, the title which Rhys preferred. Subsequent British publication by Andre Deutsch and Penguin (both in print) use *Quartet*. Page references in the text follow the Andre Deutsch edition of 1969. *Quartet* and all of Rhys's novels of the thirties are published by Vintage Books in the United States and follow the same pagination as the Deutsch hardcover editions.
2. Simone de Beauvoir, *The Second Sex* (London: Jonathan Cape, 1953), p. 65.

Chapter 4

1. Lionel Trilling, *E. M. Forster* (Norfolk, Connecticut: New Directions Books, 1943), p. 118.
2. Virginia Woolf, *The Forum*, 'Women and Fiction', *Collected Essays II* (London: The Hogarth Press, 1966), pp. 146–147.

3. Virginia Woolf, *op. cit.*, p. 148.
4. Sydney Janet Kaplan, *Feminine Consciousness in the Modern British Novel* (Urbana, Illinois: University of Illinois Press, 1975), pp. 1—2.
5. Elaine Showalter, *A Literature of Their Own, British Women Novelists from Brontë to Lessing* (Princeton, New Jersey: Princeton University Press, 1977), pp. 33—34.
6. Jean Rhys, *Voyage in the Dark* (London: Constable, 1934); *After Leaving Mr Mackenzie* (London: Jonathan Cape, 1930). All subsequent references will be to the Andre Deutsch editions of 1967 for *Voyage in the Dark* and 1969 for *Mr Mackenzie* and incorporated into the text.
7. Simone de Beauvoir, *The Second Sex*, p. 630.
8. Jean Rhys, *Good Morning, Midnight* (London: Constable, 1930), p. 38. All subsequent references will be to the Andre Deutsch edition of 1967 and will be incorporated into the text.

Chapter 5

1. Samuel Hynes, *The Auden Generation* (London: The Bodley Head, 1976).
2. Shulamith Firestone, *The Dialectic of Sex* (New York: William Morrow and Company, 1970). Cited from Bantam Book Revised edition, 1971, p. 131.

Chapter 6

1. Elgin W. Mellown, 'Character and Theme in the Novels of Jean Rhys', *Contemporary Literature*, 13, 1972, p. 470.
2. Michael Thorpe, '"The Other Side": *Wide Sargasso Sea* and *Jane Eyre*', *Ariel*, vol. 8, no. 3, July, 1977, pp. 99—110. Louis James, ed. 'Unconquerable Spirit', *Essays in West Indian Literature* (London, 1968), pp. 11—23; 'Sun Fire—Painted Fire: Jean Rhys as a Caribbean Novelist', *Ariel*, vol. 8, no. 3 July, 1977, p. 111. Dennis Porter, 'Of Heroines and Victims: Jean Rhys and *Jane Eyre*', *The Massachusetts Review*, 17, no. 3 (Autumn 1976), pp. 540—51, *passim*. Kenneth Ramchand, *The West Indian Novel and Its Background* (London, 1970), pp. 230—6. Anthony E. Luengo, '*Wide Sargasso Sea* and the Gothic Mode', *World Literature Written in English*, 15 (April, 1976), pp. 230—45.
3. See especially pp. 99—108 in Michael Thorpe.
4. My reading of *Wide Sargasso Sea* is very much opposed to Porter's throughout.
5. David Lodge, *Language of Fiction* (London: Routledge & Kegan Paul, 1966), p. 114.
6. Lionel Trilling, *The Opposing Self* (New York: The Viking Press, 1955), p. 208.
7. *Wide Sargasso Sea* (London: Deutsch, 1966), p. 17. All further references are incorporated into the text with reference to page numbers from this edition.
8. Cyril Hamshere, *The British in the Caribbean* (Cambridge, Mass.: Harvard University Press, 1972), p. 160.
9. Francis Wyndham, 'Introduction,' in *Wide Sargasso Sea*, pp. 10—11. This excellent introduction is published in the first and all subsequent editions of the novel.

Chapter 7

1. See Rosalind Miles' *The Fiction of Sex* (London, 1974) pp. 100–106. Miles offers an extensive discussion of this story.
2. *Tigers are Better-Looking* (London: Deutsch, 1968), p. 28. Subsequent references are incorporated into the text and follow this edition.
3. *Sleep It Off, Lady* (London: Deutsch, 1976), p. 16. Subsequent references are incorporated into the text and follow this edition.

Selected Bibliography

The following bibliography lists the initial British and American publication dates of Rhys's works. The secondary section is highly selective and attempts to list only the more substantial interviews and critical articles. There are a number of sources cited in the endnotes that are not repeated below, because they had only special relevance to this study. A full bibliography of both primary and secondary material, including the uncollected stories and poems, is forthcoming in the *Bulletin of Bibliography*.

I. Primary Sources

The Left Bank (Preface by Ford Madox Ford.) London: Jonathan Cape, 1927; New York: Harper and Row, 1928.

Quartet (originally published as *Postures*) London: Chatto and Windus; published as *Quartet*, New York: Simon and Schuster, 1929.

After Leaving Mr Mackenzie. London: Jonathan Cape, 1931; New York: Alfred Knopf, 1931.

Voyage in the Dark. London: Constable, 1934; New York: William Morrow and Company, 1934.

Good Morning, Midnight. London: Constable, 1930; New York: Harper and Row, 1939.

Wide Sargasso Sea. London: Andre Deutsch, 1966; New York: W. W. Dutton, 1966.

Tigers Are Better-Looking. London: Andre Deutsch, 1968; New York: Harper and Row, 1974.

Sleep It Off, Lady. London: Andre Deutsch, 1976; New York: Harper and Row, 1976.

My Day. New York: Frank Hallman, 1975.

II. Secondary Sources

Alvarez, Alfred, 'The Best Living English Novelist', *New York Times Book Review*, 17 March 1974, pp. 6–8.

Athill, Diana, 'Jean Rhys, and the Writing of *Wide Sargasso Sea*', *The Bookseller*, 3165, 20 August 1966, pp. 1378–9.

Bernstein, Marcelle, 'The Inscrutable Miss Jean Rhys', *The Observer*, 1 June 1969, pp. 40–2; 49–50.

Bowen, Stella, *Drawn From Life: Reminiscences* (London: Collins, 1941), pp. 166–8.

Burton, Peter, 'Interview', *Transatlantic Review*, 36 (Summer, 1970), pp. 105–10.

Cantwell, Mary, 'I'm a Person Without a Mask', *Mademoiselle*, 79, October, 1974, pp. 170–1.

Carter, Hannah, 'Fated to be Sad', *The Guardian*, 8 August 1968, p. 5.

Davis, Hunter, 'Rip Van Rhys', *Sunday Times* (Atticus), 6 November 1966, p. 13.

James, Louis (ed.), 'Unconquerable Spirit', in *Essays in West Indian Literature* (London: Oxford University Press, 1968), pp. 11–23.

James, Louis, 'Sun Fire–Painted Fire: Jean Rhys as a Caribbean Novelist', *Ariel*, vol. 8, no. 3 (July 1977), pp. 111–27.

Kavanagh, Julia, 'Rhys-cycled', *W*, 15 November 1974, p. 6.

Ludwig, Richard M., (ed.), *Letters of Ford Madox Ford* (Princeton: Princeton University Press, 1965), pp. 176–7.

Luengo, Anthony E., '*Wide Sargasso Sea* and the Gothic Mode', *World Literature Written in English*, 15 (April, 1976), pp. 230–45.

Mellown, Elgin, 'Character and Theme in the Novels of Jean Rhys', *Contemporary Literature*, 13 (1972), pp. 458–72.

Miles, Rosalind, *The Fiction of Sex* (New York: Barnes and Noble, 1974), pp. 96–106.

Mizener, Arthur, *The Saddest Story: A Biography of Ford Madox Ford* (New York: World Publishing Company, 1971), pp. 346–50.

Moers, Ellen, *Literary Women* (New York: Doubleday and Company, 1976), *passim*.

Petschek, Anna, 'The Shy Lady Novelist Who Went Missing for 20 Years', *Daily Express*, 1 September 1976.

Piazza, Paul, 'The World of Jean Rhys', *The Chronicle of Higher Education*, 7 March 1977, p. 19.

Porter, Dennis, 'Of Heroines and Victims: Jean Rhys and *Jane Eyre*', *The Massachusetts Review*, 17, no. 3 (Autumn, 1976), pp. 540–51.

Pree, Barry, 'Meet . . . Jean Rhys', *Observer Colour Magazine*, 3 October 1976, p. 8.

Ramchand, Kenneth, *The West Indian Novel and Its Background* (London: Faber and Faber, 1970), pp. 230—6.

Showalter, Elaine, *A Literature of Their Own* (Princeton: Princeton University Press, 1977), *passim*.

Staley, Thomas F., 'Selfhood: The Artistic Dimension', *The University of Tulsa Magazine*, 14 (Summer, 1975), pp. 12—15.

Staley, Thomas F. 'The Emergence of a Form: Style and Consciousness in Jean Rhys' *Quartet*', *Twentieth Century Literature*, 24 (Summer, 1978), pp. 202—24.

Stevens, Gini, 'Every Day is a New Day', *Radio Times*, 23—29 November 1974, p. 6.

Thorpe, Michael. '"The Other Side": *Wide Sargasso Sea* and *Jane Eyre*', *Ariel*, vol. 8, no. 3 (July, 1977), pp. 99—110.

Thurman, Judith, 'The Mistress and the Mask: Jean Rhys' Fiction', *Ms.*, 4 (January, 1976), pp. 50—4.

Vaz Dias, Selma, 'In Quest of a Missing Author', *Radio Times*, 3 May 1957, p. 25.

Webb, W. L., 'Lately Prized', *The Guardian*, 14 December 1967, p. 7.

Wyndham, Francis, 'Introduction to Jean Rhys' *The London Magazine*, 7 (January, 1960), pp. 15—18. (Reprinted as the introduction to *Wide Sargasso Sea*.)

Wyndham, Francis, 'A Stark Reserve' *Sunday Times*, 17 December 1967, p.26.

Index